THE CELTIC CAKERS

PAGE 16

PAGE 28

PAGE 52

PAGE 40

PAGE 68

acknowledgements

There are a good few people who helped make this book possible whom I need to thank. This book was a huge undertaking (more than I was expecting), but thankfully, I'm lucky to have supportive, talented friends with some very special skills.

I need to give a big mention to two ladies in particular who have worked very hard with me from the start. They made sure that everything produced in this book was up to snuff and put together professionally. They scoured through each tutorial multiple times, and I owe them a huge thanks. So, Shirín Nagle, my proofreader, and Jay Istvanffy, my editor, thank you so much! This book would not have come together so well without you.

To all of my friends who contributed to this book, I thank you. You stepped up, dealt with my incessant pushing of deadlines, awkward photo demands, and queries. You all provided brilliant tutorials that you should be proud of. I know I am.

Thank you to my husband, Barry, who planted the idea of this book in my brain in the first place. He very patiently picked up the slack with the family and house while I had to hide away on my computer or in my cake room to finish just 'one more thing'. He still managed to support me and to help out where he could. To my kids and potential budding decorators, a big thank you for understanding the time that it takes to put something like this together and for the constant cuddles.

To my photographer, Brad Anderson of www.photoone.ie, who spent a long and rainy day on the streets of Galway getting new profile photos geared for me for this book. The results are brilliant, and you got that Galway vibe to shine through despite the weather.

There are so many other people who lent an ear and offered advice who need to get a mention too. Jill Holtz of Mykidstime.ie with her marketing knowledge. Avital Dines who always gives an honest opinion. Heather McGrath and Kelli Elkadri for getting me out of a bind. Avalon Yarnes, Melanie Underwood, and Mairín O'Reilly who offered their knowledge, and support and who let me whinge to them on occasion.

THE CELTIC CAKERS

For Mia & Cormac

Table
of contents

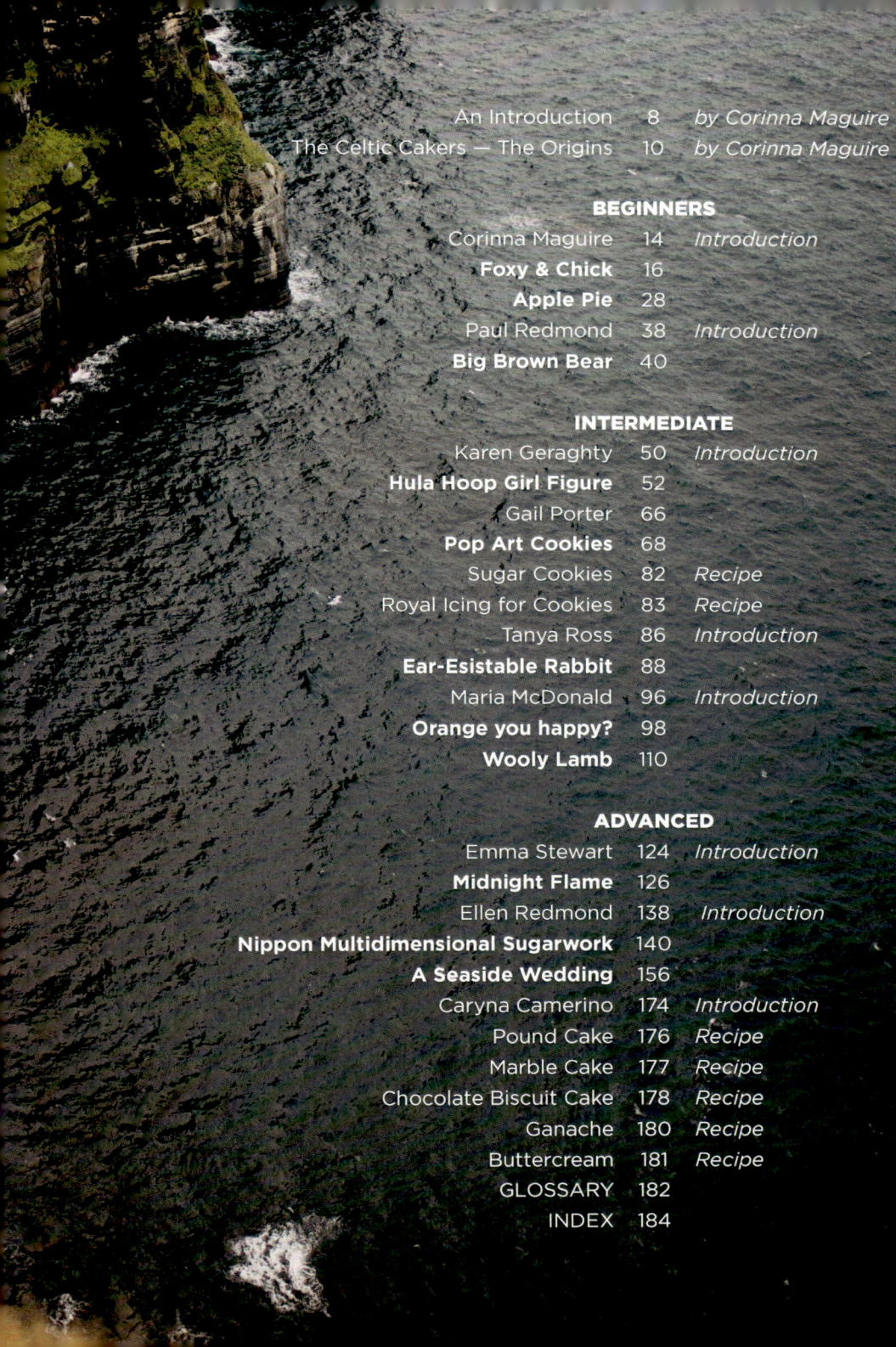

An introduction

Writing a cake tutorial book has been on my mind for a good while. I was originally a graphic designer, and a tutorial book seemed like something that I could put together on my own. But after a while, I thought it might be fun to include some of my cake friends from around Ireland to join in this book adventure. Things are more fun when you share them anyway, right?! So, I asked some of them to join me in putting together this 'Celtic Cakers' photo tutorial book for you. I would have loved to include more cake decorators, but there is only so much space. Who knows, maybe there will be a second edition!

I've always been proud of the talent in Ireland. For such a small country, I think the standard here is amazing, and you can see this at the competitions and shows. I'm thrilled to be able to compile and showcase just a small part of their art in this book.

Not all of the people included in this book are Irish born and bred, but I still consider them all to be Irish at heart. I myself left Ireland when I was four and grew up in Alberta, Canada. After I finished college, I came back to Ireland for a 'holiday' — a holiday that turned into 18 years of living here! So although some of these people's roots might not have started in Ireland, their roots have grown here, just like my own.

My goal for this book was for it to be as varied as possible and to not just show one technique or style. Instead, I wanted to illustrate everything from piping to modelling, carved cakes to sugar flowers, and even a bit of painting. Some of those things I myself can't do or haven't done!

Choosing who would join me in this adventure was not easy. I approached some of my incredibly talented friends whom I've known since I started my cake journey.

To begin with, I contacted my award-winning friend, Tanya Ross (Novel-T Cakes), who has offered insight into creating a beautiful carved rabbit. I've known Tanya since I began teaching cakes, and she's become my partner in crime over the years.

The incredibly funny, intelligent, and talented Karen Geraghty (Bake Cake Create) has some serious figure modelling skills. She's another good friend and has to be one of the most supportive cakers out there, not to mention that she's always up for a laugh.

The punk of the cake world, Paul Redmond, shares my love of creepy cakes. I actually have to credit him for introducing me to the cake world in Ireland. After meeting him at my first Dublin cake show, he invited me to join my first collaboration in Dublin, 'The Cake Dahls'.

I have known Gail Porter, the cookie whisperer, since I started teaching cake decorating. She has slowed down with her orders these days, so I was thrilled when she said that she'd take part in this book.

Ellen Redmond works with very detailed bas-relief and painting. Her cakes are so intricate that I could stare at them all day and still see something new.

Emma Stewart is our one caker from Northern Ireland. She is an award-winning wedding cake designer. Her work is beautiful, and she is a warm, modest person.

Maria McDonald has such a fun and quirky style, and it shows here in her Orange tutorial. Her cakes caught my attention a couple of years ago, and I've been a big fan of her work ever since. This is all the more amazing given that she is the mum of six-year-old triplets.

Last but not least comes the other Canadian, Caryna. Our paths crossed a few years ago in the strangest of circumstances (read her bio) and a camaraderie began. Her award-winning bakery is one of the tastiest places in Dublin, and I was thrilled that she agreed to offer a few recipes for our book collaboration.

The 'Celtic Cakers' book is meant to be a guide to not only create the cakes themselves, but to learn the techniques that these talented people have shown. I'm honoured to be the one to compile this work, and I hope you enjoy reading it as much as I did making it.

Happy caking!

Corinna Maguire

The Spanish Arch, Galway City
Photograph by Photo One Studios www.photoone.ie

The Celtic Cakers
the origins

I've called this book The 'Celtic Cakers', but I have to give credit to the name and where it originated. Two years ago, I was a small part of a huge collaboration, 'Away with the Fairies,' at the Dublin Sugarcraft Cake Competition.

The collaboration was the brainchild of Breda O'Brien and Phillip Mullen to organise a life-sized fairy wonderland. A group of Irish cakers were involved in putting it together in time for the show. We named ourselves the 'Celtic Cakers'. We were in charge of building trees, making leaves and the backdrop, and creating animals to be set among the fairies, including a swan, rabbit, badger, and stag (it was huge!).

An even larger group of international cake friends joined in the whole experience by shipping in over 200 individual fairies from every corner of the world.

The project wasn't without a few bumps in the road as a good few of the fairies were damaged in transit. There were so many breakages that a fairy hospital was created, with people repairing all of the injured fairies around the clock. For a while, it didn't look like there was enough time to finish the project. But everyone, and I mean everyone, stepped up to help us finish it all on time. Exhausted but happy, we made it happen.

In the end, the result was incredible. Just watching the smiling faces as people gazed, transfixed, at the display was reward enough. You wouldn't be able to look twice at the showpiece without seeing something different or finding a new fairy tucked away somewhere. I'm incredibly proud to say that I was a part of the whole project.

I hope that in some way, the title of this book will help to keep the Celtic Cakers name alive.

"Ever tried. Ever failed. No matter.
Try Again. Fail again. Fail better."
Samuel Beckett

BEGINNER
TUTORIALS

Corinna Maguire

Lovin' from the Oven — Oranmore, Co. Galway

'When I grow up I want to be a cake decorator'... are words that never came out of my mouth as a child. I've worked at a multitude of things: musician, McDonald's mascot, teacher's assistant, photographer, graphic designer ... the list goes on. But it was only when I had my first child that I tried my hand with over-the-top birthday cakes. Friends started asking for wedding cakes and cakes for their kids' parties. And then the competitions happened.

After some wins and even a disqualification, there was no turning back. I was addicted and had to do more!

Although I was born in Gorey, Co. Wexford, Ireland, I actually grew up in Alberta, Canada, from the age of four until I was around 22. After college, I came on holidays to visit Ireland and instantly fell in love with Galway. With it's fun-loving people, street musicians, scenery, and the general buzz around town, I knew I had to stay. So my 'holiday' turned into living here, and I wouldn't think of leaving, even on the horrible rainy days.

After we married, my husband and I moved out to Oranmore, a beautiful seaside village outside of Galway. It's a slower pace out here, but it suits me perfectly, and it's a great place for our kids to grow up.

I now work from home making the occassional cake for events, teaching classes locally and internationally, and offering online tutorials.

The Long Walk seen from the Claddagh, Galway City
Photograph by Photo One Studios www.photoone.ie

Foxy & chick

by Corinna Maguire

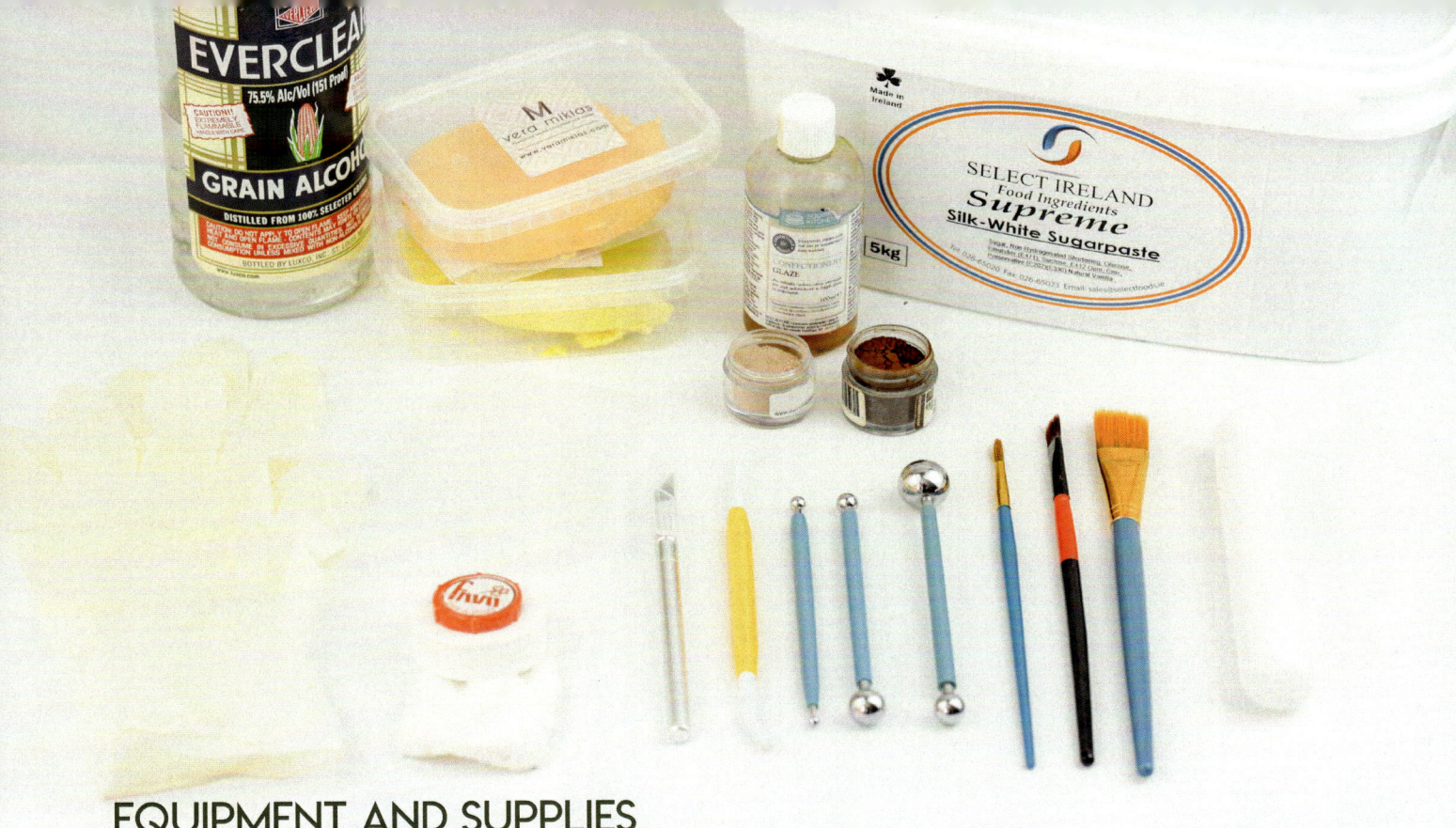

EQUIPMENT AND SUPPLIES

	9" cake (3" high)
	6" cake (5" high)
	10" cake board
700g/25oz	Ganache
500g/18oz	Buttercream
200g/7oz	Ivory fondant *(Select Ireland)*
	- white mixed with a little brown and chestnut gel colours
800g/28oz	Burnt orange fondant *(Select Ireland)*
	- red and yellow fondant mixed with a small amount of brown
140g/5oz	Dark green fondant
10g/0.5oz	Black fondant
	White modelling chocolate coloured yellow *(Vera Miklas™)*
	White modelling chocolate coloured orange *(Vera Miklas™)*
	High-alcohol vodka

100g/3.5oz	Rice cereal treats
	Corn flour
	Duster to hold corn flour
	Spaghetti strand
	Medium fluffy paintbrush
	Medium flat paintbrush
	Small flat paintbrush
	Rolling pin
	Knife
	Blade/X-Acto® knife
	Flexi smoother
	Palette knife
	Large ball tool
	Medium ball tool
	Small ball tool
	Dresden tool *(veiner tool)*
	Disposable gloves
	Mushroom-coloured petal dust
	Brown petal dust

1

Take your 8" cake and, using the 6" cake tin as a guide, mark a 6" circle on one of the edges.

2

Follow the mark and cut out the 6" section of cake. Remove this inside piece and save it for later.

3

Place the ring of cake onto the cake board and secure it into place with some buttercream.

4

Round the inside edge of the outer ring of cake. This edge will eventually become your fox's tail.

5

Place your first layer of cake into the centre of the ring.

6

Coat each layer with buttercream and place the next cake on top. I made a mix of chocolate and vanilla layers, but any cakes will do.

Corinna Maguire — www.lovinfromtheoven.ie

7 Keep layering the 6" cakes until you reach about 7" in height. Cut off a section of the outer ring so that more of the fox's body will be seen.

8 To round out the base of the outer ring, carve off a small triangular section.

9 Carve off any edges that you see so that it's fully rounded.

10 Carve off 2 angled pieces from the top and round off any sharp edges.

11 Coat the cake with a layer of ganache. Also add some ganache in the crease where the tail and the body attach.

12 A flexi smoother is handy for 'ganaching' round shapes.

Work some rice cereal treats into a wide cone shape about 2.5 inches wide.

Coat the rice cereal treat cone with ganache. I find this easier to do using a chopstick pierced into the treat.

Paste some more ganache onto the base of the cutout section and secure the snout into place.

Using a gloved finger or a small spoon, blend in the seam around the snout with more ganache.

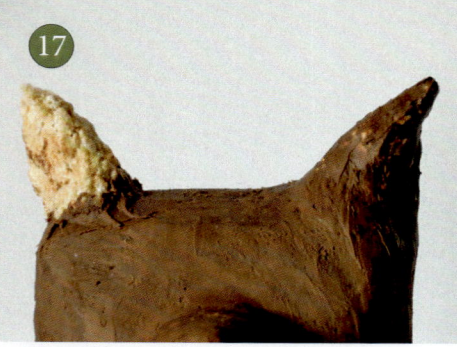

To make the 2 ears with narrow rice cereal treat cones, repeat the process. Attach the ears with ganache and coat with ganache as before.

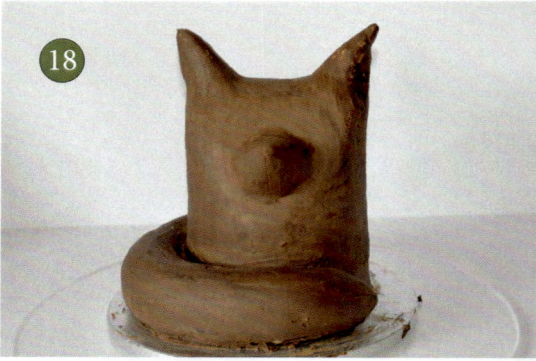

Using flexi smoothers or a gloved hand, blend in the seams until the ears are flush with the fox's body. Lightly wet the surface.

Roll out a piece of burnt orange fondant large enough to cover the fox's body. Dust with corn flour and roll it up. Starting from the back or side, unroll it around the body.

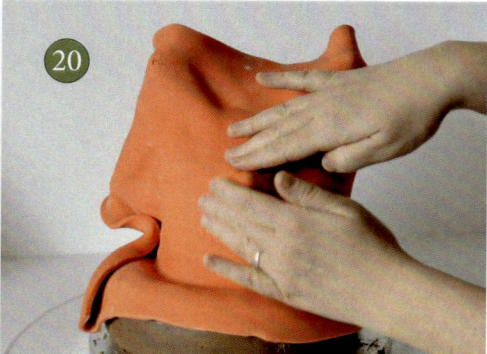

Secure the fondant onto the nose first so that it doesn't tear. Gently rub the fondant, making sure that it's fully attached to the 'ganached' cake.

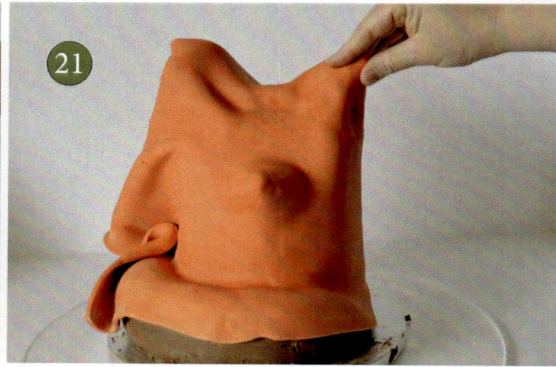

Repeat with the rest of the fox's body and up around the ears. Pinch the excess fondant together at the cake's surface on the top and sides.

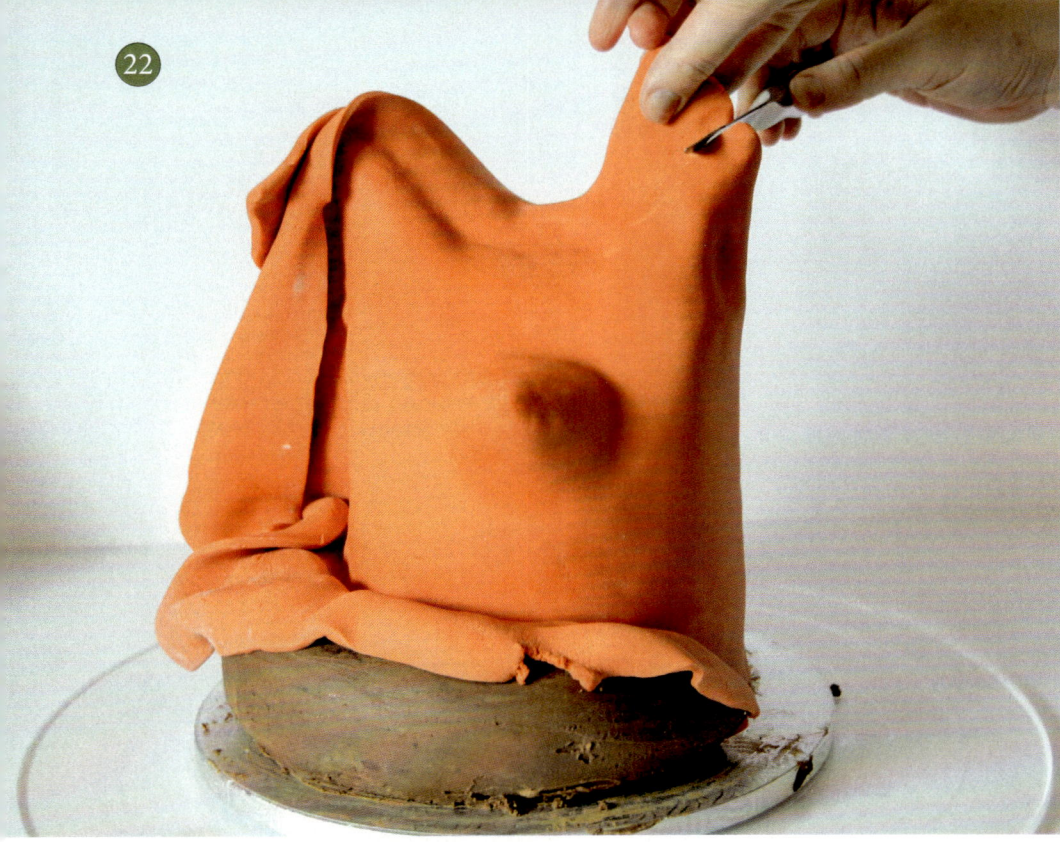

You may need a small dab of water to secure the 2 sides of excess fondant together. Once secured, carefully cut off the excess fondant of the top, side, and base.

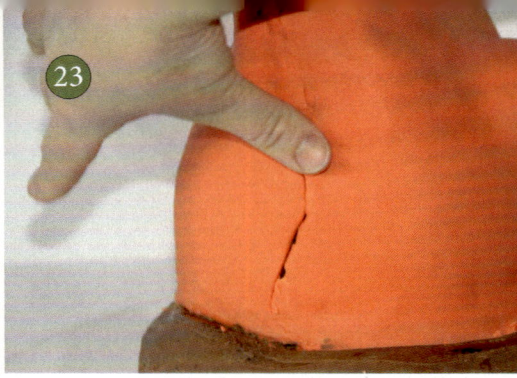

Using water and a twist of your thumb, blend in the seams with clean hands. Flexi smoothers are also great for getting rid of seams.

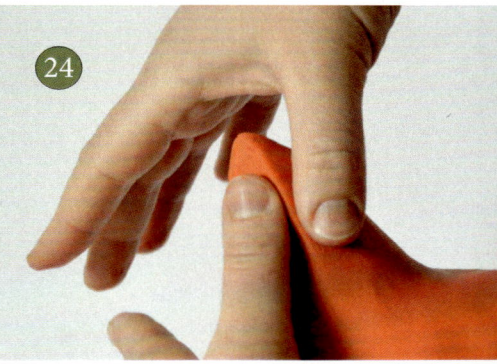

Mould the ears to shape by pinching an edge out of the fondant with your hands.

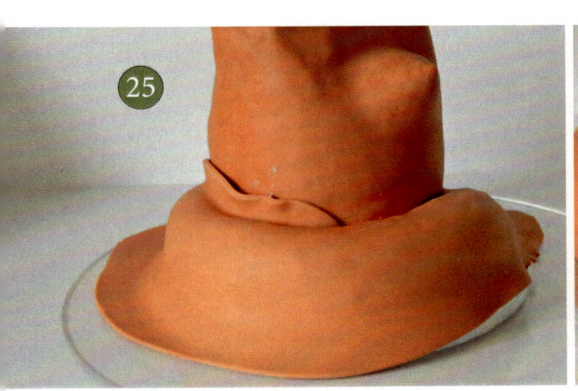

Lightly wet the ganached tail. Roll out another long section of fondant and cover the fox's tail.

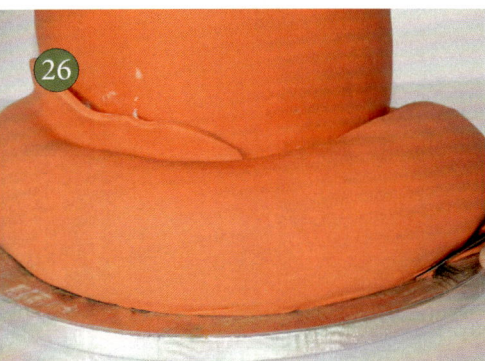

Using a sharpened dowel or dry paintbrush, tuck the fondant in to the top and base of the tail and cover the ganache. Cut off the excess.

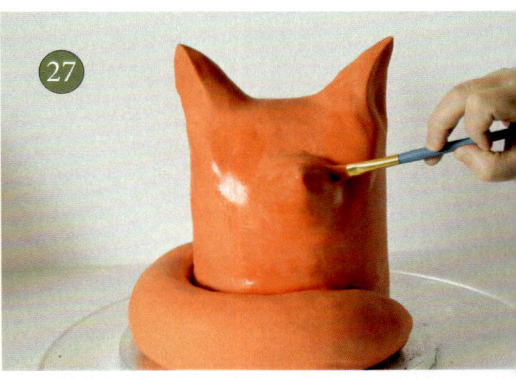

Using the template at the end of this tutorial as a guide, cut out the fox's face and belly with ivory fondant. Wet the base of the snout, eye areas, and belly.

28 Starting at the tip of the snout, secure the ivory fondant into place. Make sure the edges are neat and even. To even out the edges, drag the Dresden tool along the seams.

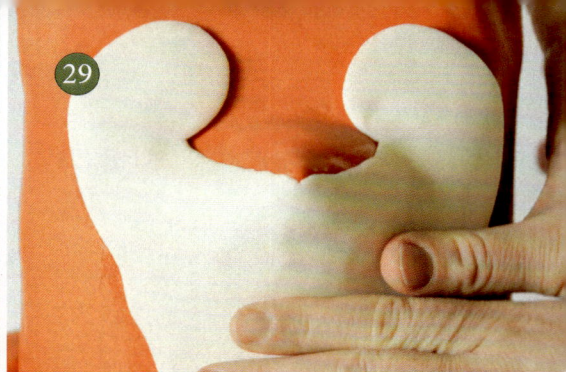

29 Smooth out any marks you've made and paint in along any edges that aren't fully attached to the cake.

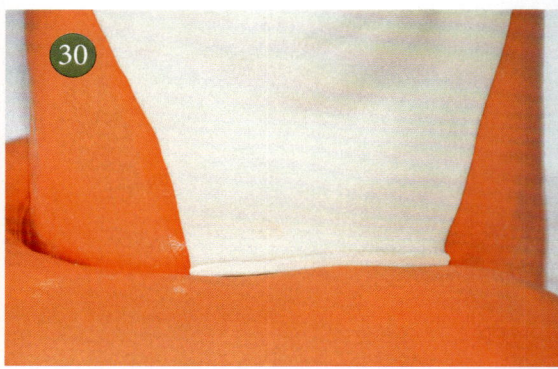

30 Push the ivory fondant into the crease between the tail and body and cut off the excess.

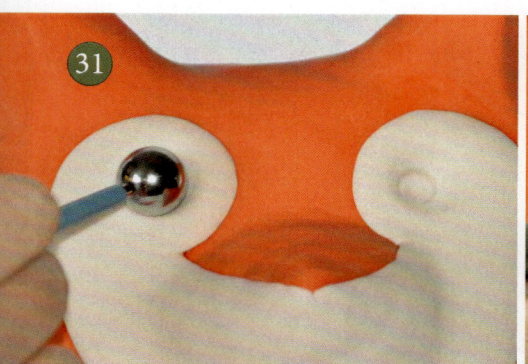

31 Use a large ball tool to make indents for the eyes.

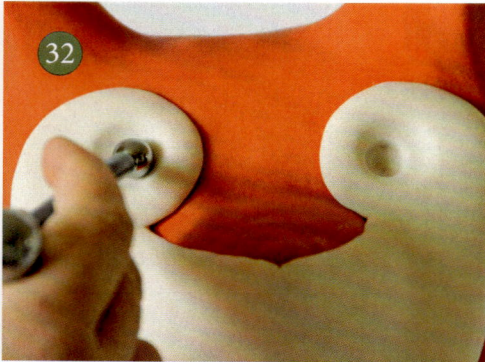

32 Use a medium ball tool to indent the centres of the larger indents. This indent is where you will place the eyes.

33 Using the side of a small spatula or the sharp side of the Dresden tool, make a vertical indent from the tip of the nose to the base.

To make the fox's mouth, use the same Dresden tool to make a horizontal indentation at the base of the vertical indentation.

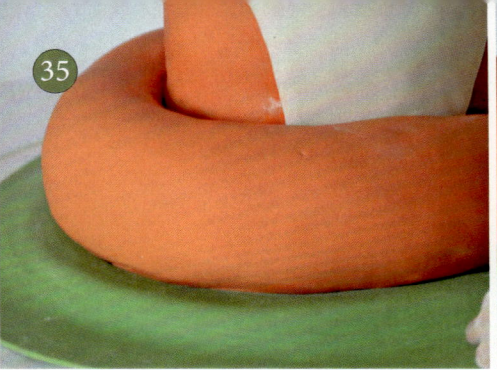

Roll out a long section of green fondant. Lightly wet the cake drum and push the green fondant into place, making sure the board is fully covered. Cut off the excess.

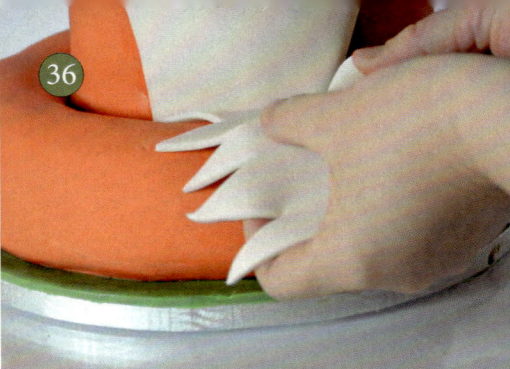

Use the tail template at the end of this tutorial to cut out another piece of ivory fondant. Lightly wet the end of the tail and secure the fondant into place.

Push the ivory fondant into the creases and cut off the excess. Make sure that the seams are tucked in well and not visible.

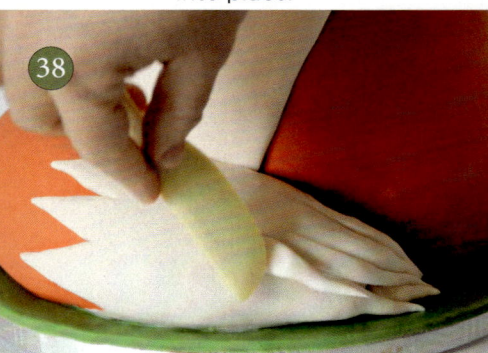

OPTIONAL — If you want to give the tail more flow, attach tapered sausages of ivory paste to the end.

To give the hairs movement, blend in the thick end of each sausage and bend them.

Add a few extra strokes of 'fur' to the ivory fondant.

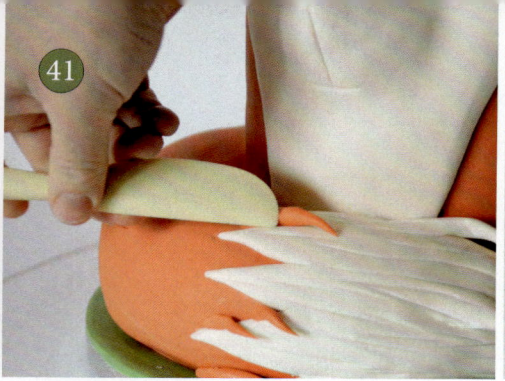

Add a few more pieces of the burnt orange fondant and overlap them with the ivory.

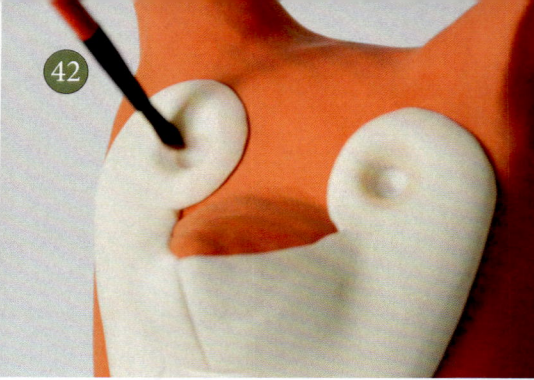

With almost no dust on your brush, dust a little mushroom-coloured petal dust into the larger eye indentations.

With barely any dust on your brush, dust a little more mushroom-coloured petal dust into the creases on the fox's snout and mouth. Less is more—dusting these sections will just make them more noticeable.

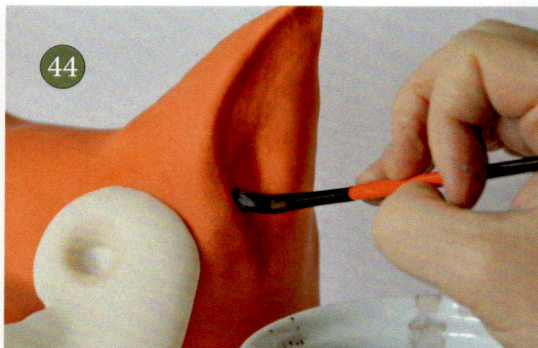

Mix a little brown petal dust with some high-alcohol vodka and paint a section inside the front of the ear to create some depth.

Roll a grape-sized ball of black fondant into a teardrop shape.

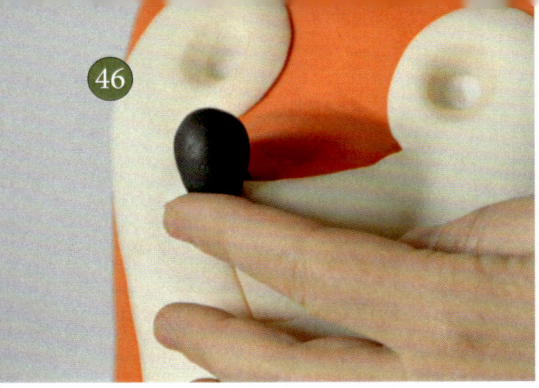

46 Attach this piece to the pointed end of the snout. Hold it in place until it's fully secure.

47 To support the nose, push it slightly back onto the snout.

48 Roll 2 equal balls of black fondant the same size as the holes that you made before. Attach into place with a dab of water.

49 To create a highlight, roll 2 tiny bits of white fondant (or ivory) and place them on the top left corner of each eye with some water.

50 Once dry, paint some confectioner's glaze over the nose and eyeballs. This technique brings creatures to life.

51 To create the chick, roll a ball of yellow modelling chocolate to around 1.5" in diameter.

52 Add a small triangle of orange modelling chocolate to the top one-third of the yellow ball.

53 Make 2 little triangles and attach them to the sides of the ball with a little water.

54 Using the small ball tool, make 2 indentations just above the beak. Fill with 2 equally sized black balls.

(55)

Place a couple of bits of yellow to the top of the head for downy tufts.

(56)

Roll a sausage of orange modelling paste and attach it to the base of the chick.

(57)

Add 3 more small sausages to the ends of the legs.

(58)

Now you have a simple little chick! You may want to remove the legs while you attach the chick onto the fox.

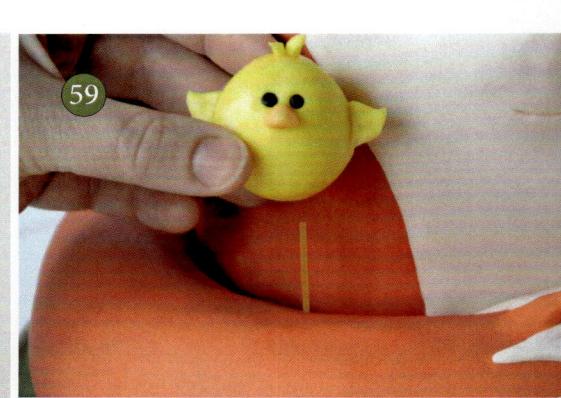

(59)

Attach the chick to the fox's tail, securing the chick into place with a bit of spaghetti.

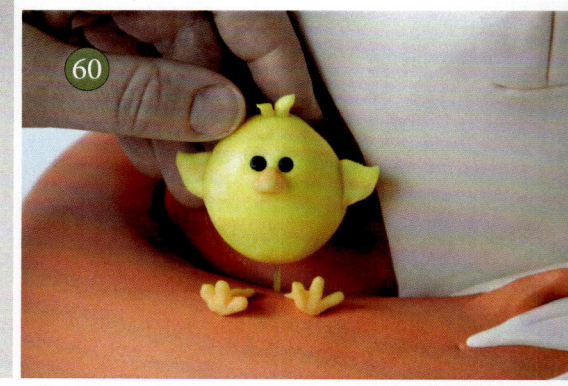

(60)

Once you know where the chick will sit, place the legs using a bit of water to secure them.

Corinna Maguire — www.lovinfromtheoven.ie

FOX *TEMPLATES*

Use these templates as a general guide to recreate the fox cake. Photocopy the templates to a percentage that will suit your own cake size. Or create your own version using these as inspiration.

Apple Pie Cake
by Corinna Maguire

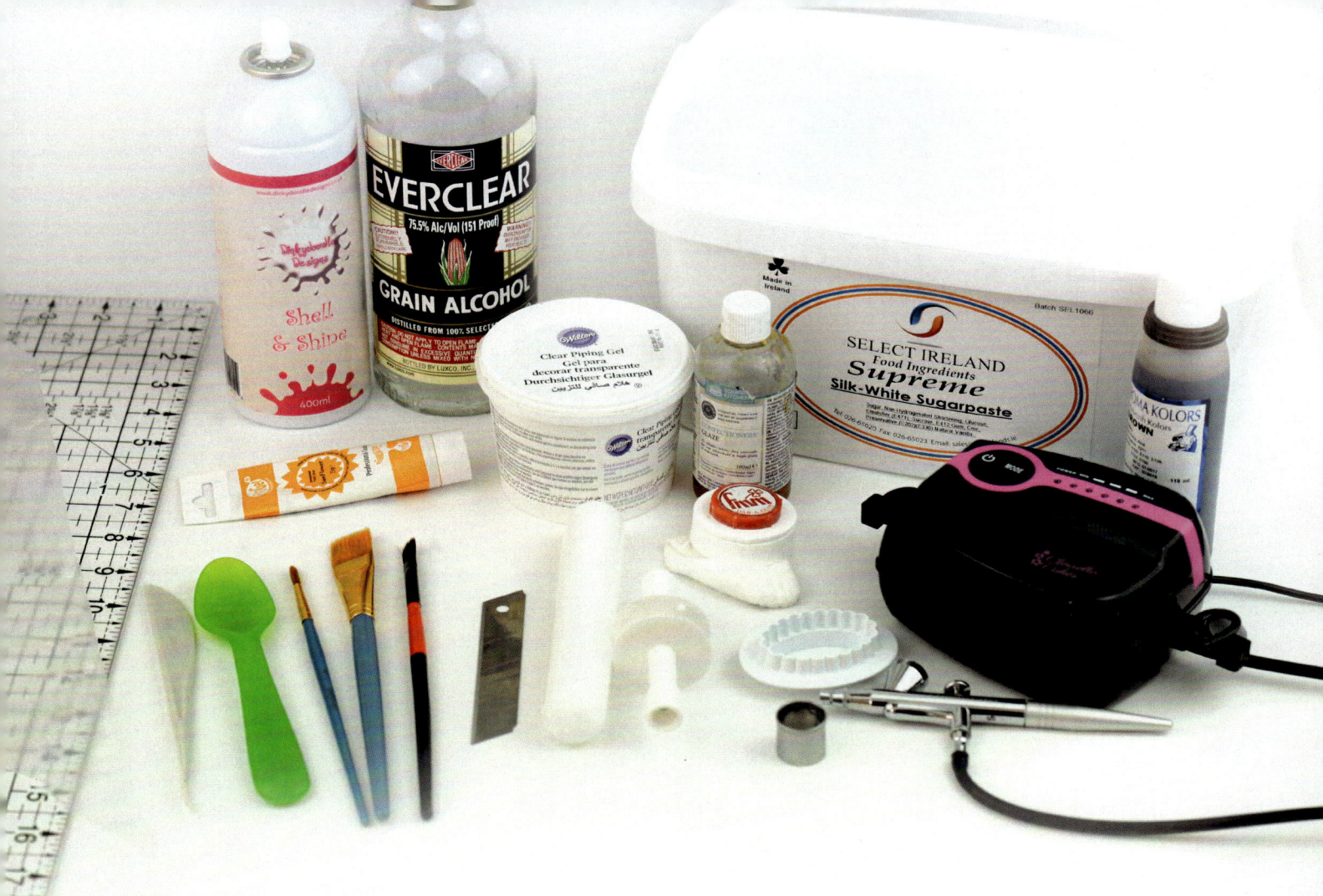

EQUIPMENT AND SUPPLIES

1x		8" cake	
1x		8" cake board	
1x		14" cake drum	
95g/3 cups		Milk chocolate ganache	
1700g/60oz		White fondant	
		(Select Ireland)	
700g/25oz		Red fondant	
		(Select Ireland)	
		Florist paste	

Sunflower colouring gel
(ProGel®)
200g/7oz Piping gel
Cinnamon
200g/7oz Royal icing
Corn flour
Paint brushes
Oval cutter *(1.5" x 1")*
Rolling pin
Ribbon cutter

Fork
Airbrush
Don't have an airbrush?
It's ok—you can use edible petal dust!
Brown airbrush colour
Dark brown dust
Edible silver lustre dust
Confectioner's glaze
Tin foil/aluminium foil
Spoon

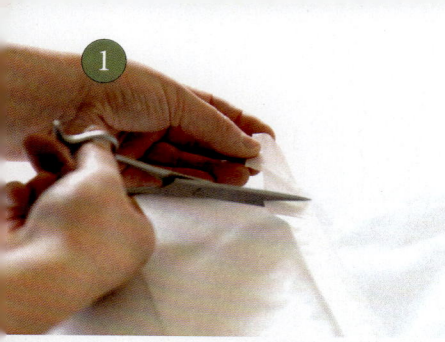

1 Cut a long strip of baking parchment around 26" x 6" inches. Fold over a 1" lip length-wise. Cut slits into the fold along the full length.

2 Coat an 8" cake tin with shortening to secure the parchment paper in place. Wrap the paper around the edges with the slits on the base. Cut another circular piece to cover the tin's base.

3 Bake your cake and carve the top into shape, keeping a slightly domed peak in the centre top.

4 Slice the cake into 2 layers.

5 Fill the cake with your filling of choice. I used a milk chocolate ganache. Secure the cake onto an 8" cake board with another bit of ganache.

6 Cover the cake with milk chocolate ganache. This is my 'go-to' to cover a cake as it's delicious and gives the cake a firmer exterior, helping to hold its shape.

7 Cut out a slice of the cake. You need to work inside the cut-out slice, so make sure the angle is wide enough.

8 Coat with ganache the cut-out area and the slice taken out. I sometimes use a chopstick to hold small pieces of cake in place when coating.

9 Smooth out the edges and make sure that there isn't any cake still exposed.

Corinna Maguire — www.lovinfromtheoven.ie

Colour some florist paste with a tiny amount of sunflower gel colour until you have the 'inside of an apple' colour.

Roll out the florist paste reasonably thick. These will be your apple slices.

Use an oval cutter to start cutting out the apple slices. Cut these pieces into large and small sections for the random apple slices.

Colour some fondant with the sunflower gel colour but in a slightly darker shade than the 'apple slices'. Use it to cover the inside edges of the main cake.

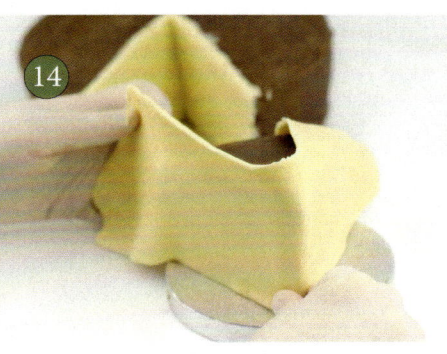

Use the sunflower-coloured fondant to cover the 2 inside slice sides of the piece that you cut out.

Cover the tops of each section of cake and blend in the seams.

Make a mix of piping gel, sunflower gel colour, and some cinnamon shavings. Paint a layer on top of your cakes.

Attach some of the 'apple slices' to the top of the piping gel and coat again over the top.

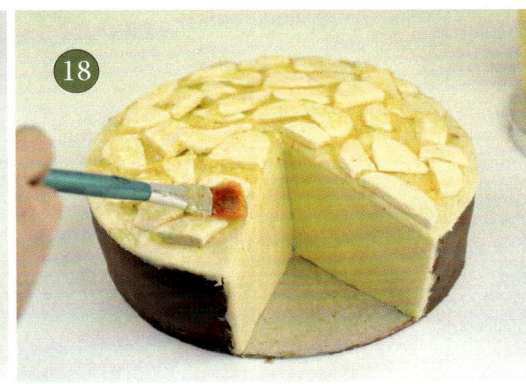

Repeat on the large cake and paint in between each of the 'apple slices', filling in all of the gaps with piping gel.

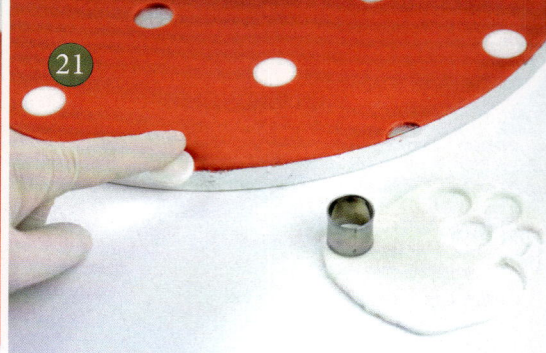

19 Coat a 14" cake drum with red fondant and use a blade to cut off the excess fondant from the edges, as you would with a pie crust.

20 Mark the board every 3" as a guide for where to cut out the polka-dots. A transparent quilting ruler is handy for cake moments like this.

21 Use a small circle cutter on each of the marks and fill them with corresponding white fondant dots. Secure each circle into place with a small dab of water.

22 Cut off any fondant that extends past the board.

23 Place the cake on the board. To cover the exposed cake board add a triangle of white fondant to the cut-out section of cake. To make it look as though the filling is sliding down, add some segments of apples and coat again with the piping gel mix.

24 Roll out a length of white fondant, long enough to wrap around the cake. Use dowels to keep the thickness even.

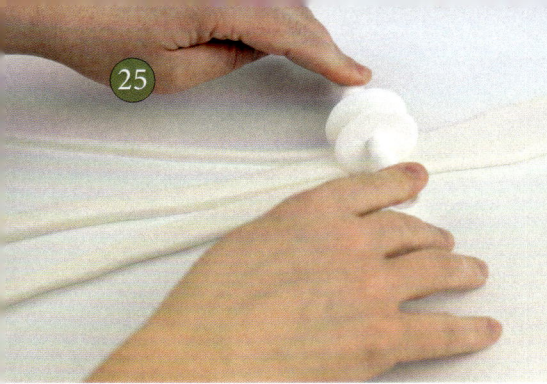

Use a ribbon cutter to cut out an even band of white fondant.

Wrap the white fondant band around the edge of the pie to be the 'plate edge'.

Colour fondant with some sunflower gel and a bit of brown. Roll out a strip, long and wide enough to wrap around the 'pie'.

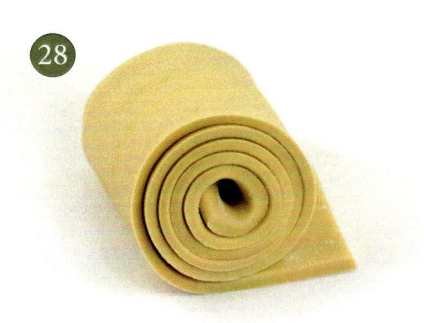

Cut off the excess and dust generously with some corn flour. Roll up the strip to make it easier to apply to the cake.

Lightly wet the sides of the cake and unroll the long strip around the edges. Make sure that the base is flush with the 'plate'. Cut off any excess fondant.

Cut off the excess from the top of the strip, keeping it even with the top of the cake.

Roll out a large piece of the light brown fondant and use the strip cutter to cut sections 0.6" (1.5cm) long.

Get a large piece of acetate. Or if you're like me and only have smaller sheets, join 2 pieces together with some tape.

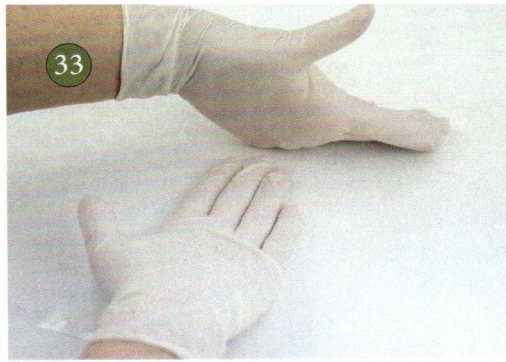

Grease the acetate with a little shortening to make it easier to place the woven top for your pie crust.

Lay out the vertical strips, alternating over and under a crossing horizontal strip. Keep gaps between the strips so that the filling will show through.

Lift every second vertical strip and place a crossing horizontal strip. Fold back the vertical ones. Alternate and repeat.

Continue until the weave is complete and large enough to cover the pie. Secure each crossover by painting a little water on the joins.

Lift the acetate with the woven fondant and place carefully over top of the 'apples'.

Try and get it down on the first try, as the piping-gel apples are quite sticky.

Carefully remove the acetate without ruining the woven fondant.

Using a sharp blade, carefully cut out the gap where you removed the pie slice. Save this cutout to place on the cake wedge.

Cut away the excess woven fondant from the edges.

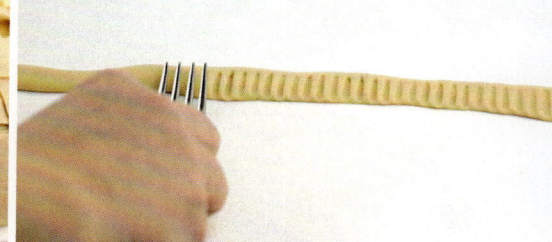

Roll out another strip of fondant and use a fork to mark along the length of the fondant.

 Corinna Maguire — www.lovinfromtheoven.ie

43 Attach this strip to the join of the woven fondant and the sides. Use a tool to blend in this seam and secure it into place.

44 Bend and push the edges of the crust to make it more uneven and natural.

45 Roll a flat-edged tool over the seam under the side crust to blend it in to the sides of the pie.

46 Use the fork to deepen any markings on the crust that have been rubbed out.

47 Use some tin foil (aluminium foil) to create texture on the top and the sides of the full cake and the slice too.

48 Use an airbrush and brown colour to darken the raised parts of the top to make the pie look 'baked'.

49 Airbrush the edges of the pie crust too. This effect can also be done using a fluffy brush and some brown dust.

50 With a fluffy brush and dark brown edible petal dust, darken small areas on the top of the pie to make them look more cooked.

51 Using a metal dessert spoon, scoop out a ball of white fondant.

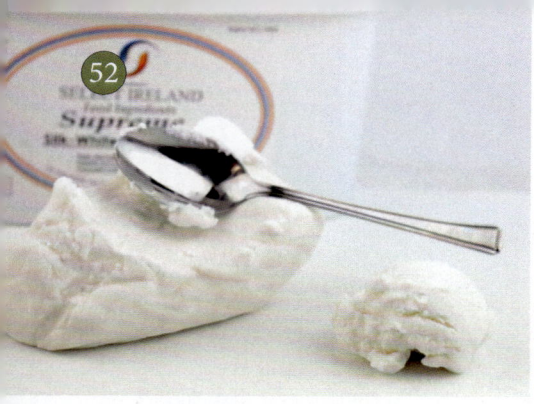

52 It might take a few scoops until you're happy with a piece that looks like a scoop of ice cream.

53 Drizzle royal icing (as thick as honey) on the pie slice, and drip it over the edges in an area just slightly bigger than the scoop of fondant.

54 While the royal icing is still wet, place the fondant ball on the top.

55 Blend in the wet royal icing to the base of the lump of ice cream. Allow the royal icing to crust over and dry.

56 Once the royal icing has dried and crusted over, some of its shine will be gone. Paint over it with some edible glaze to add shine.

57 Thinly roll out some florist paste and cover a corn flour-dusted spoon. Cut to shape using the spoon as a guide.

58 Once the spoon has fully hardened, use a sharp blade to carefully remove any pieces that stick out.

59 Mix some edible silver lustre dust with high-alcohol vodka and paint onto the spoon to give a silver effect.

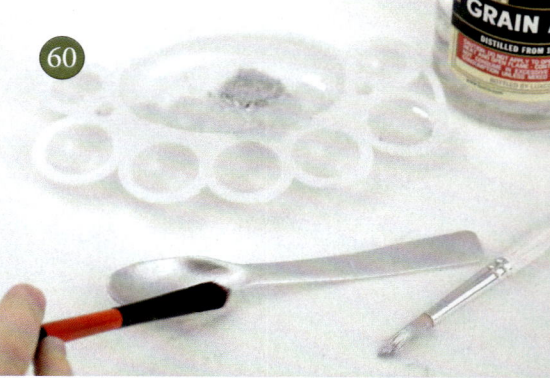

60 Before it has fully dried, dust the spoon using a second fluffy brush with some dry edible lustre dust.

61

Once dried, repeat the process of painting and dusting on the back side of the spoon. Pay attention to the edges.

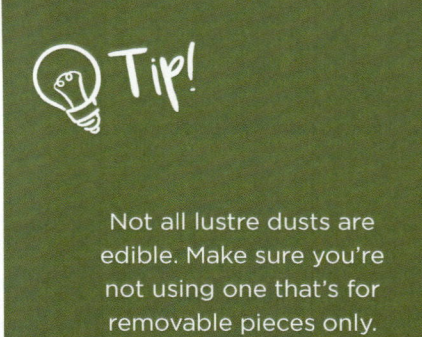

Tip!

Not all lustre dusts are edible. Make sure you're not using one that's for removable pieces only.

62

Once fully dried, you can spray or paint some edible glaze onto the spoon.

63

Place the spoon on the board and drizzle some more of the piping gel mix with apple slices onto the spoon. To finish off the board, glue a ribbon around its edge. Add a few more drips, and your apple pie cake is done!

Paul REDMOND

Purple Feather — Dublin City Centre

I've been decorating cakes for over 30 years—from covering my parents' kitchen in icing sugar as a teenager to supplying all the top shops in London in the early 90s. On my return to Ireland, I took a break from a career in engineering to run the decorating floor of a large bakery. Since then, I've started my own company, Purple Feather Cake Design, which I run from a purpose-built, light-filled home studio where I get to play without disturbing the rest of my family. I particularly like to use my engineering background to make gravity-defying and unusual creations.

I've lived in Dublin for most of my life and have settled in the city centre, overlooking the famous Royal Canal (where the 'aul triangle went jingle jangle') and in the shadow of the national stadium, Croke Park. I love the location for its proximity to everything the city has to offer while being minutes from the sea and some great parks. But mainly I love that the area is packed full of creative, interesting, and passionate people.

Looking to the future, I intend to keep pushing boundaries with my cakes, entering competitions. and collaborating with other decorators from around the world as often as possible.

THE BIG BROWN
BEAR
by Paul Redmond

EQUIPMENT AND SUPPLIES

15cm/6"	Polystyrene egg
5cm/2"	Polystyrene ball
	Cake dummy to work on
	6" Cake drum
	Wooden skewer
300g/10.5oz	Dark modelling chocolate
300g/10.5oz	White sugarpaste
160g/5.5oz	Green sugarpaste
90g/3oz	Black sugarpaste
30g/1oz	Grey sugarpaste
10g/.5oz	Red sugarpaste
10g/.5oz	Yellow sugarpaste
	Black liquid colour
2x	6mm white dragées
	Confectioner's varnish
	Flower sprinkles
	Florist wire
	Rolling pin
	Knife
	Medium brushes
	Fine brushes
	Dresden tool
	Ball tool
	Dish brush
	Material impression mat
	Smoother
	Stitching wheel
4cm	Circle cutter
6cm	Circle cutter
	Small flower cutter

1

Skewer the 15cm polystyrene egg to a dummy for stability. Apply a thin layer of piping gel to the egg and cover it with the modelling chocolate.

2

Use another wooden skewer to attach a 5cm polystyrene ball to the top of the egg. Cover with the modelling chocolate, letting the excess drape down to fill the neck.

3

Smooth down the neck area, blending with a dampened finger.

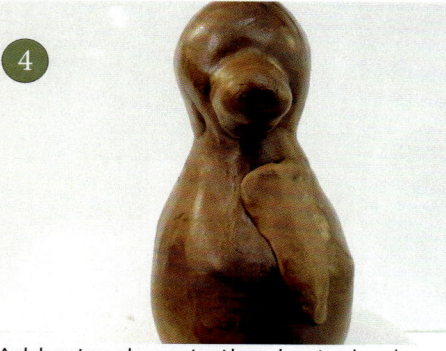

4

Add extra shape to the chest, cheeks, and tail. Add the snout. Using the fat end of the Dresden tool and a slightly dampened finger, smooth it all.

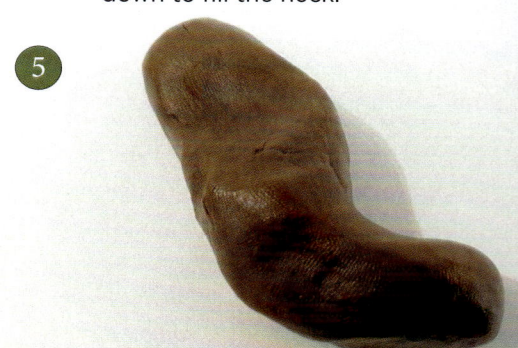

5

For each of the rear legs, form L shapes from 60g of the 50/50 mix. Flatten the tops of the legs to allow for where they join the body. Attach the legs with a small bit of water.

6

For each of the front legs, use 35g of the 50/50 mix. To give the bear life and movement, place the legs in slightly different positions.

7

To make the ears, take 2 pea-sized pieces of modelling chocolate and flatten them into an oval.

8

Curl the flattened ears into a dome and attach them with a drop of water, if needed.

9

Using a ball tool, make the eye sockets and indent the forehead a little.

10

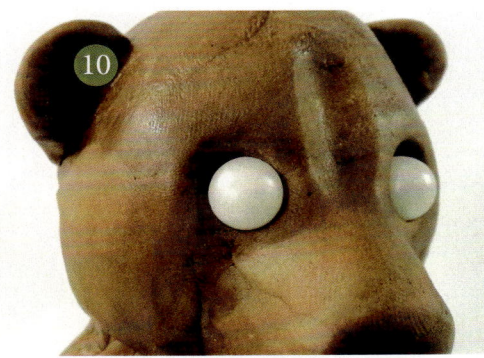

To make the eyeballs, push 2 x 6mm white dragées well into the sockets.

11

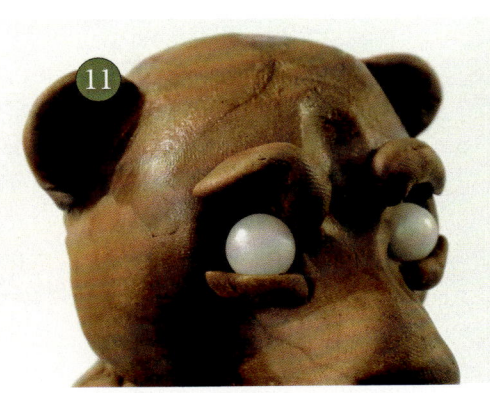

Roll 2cm x 1cm long sausages for above the eyes and slightly smaller sausages for underneath.

12

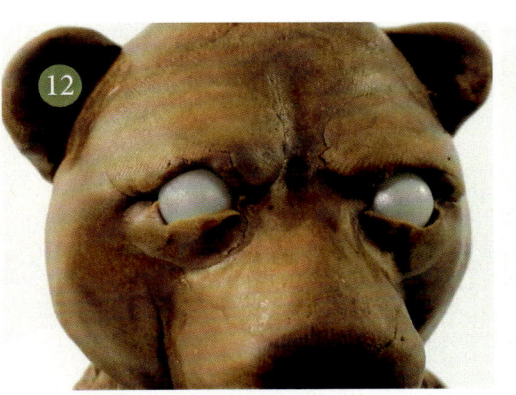

Smooth out the sausages, bringing them up and down a little to slightly cover the eyes.

13

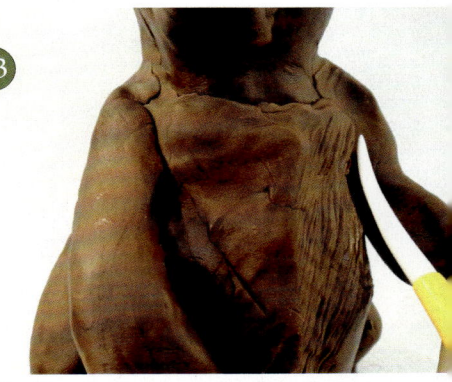

Starting in the centre of the chest and working down and out, use a Dresden tool to mark the fur, stroking the surface with the back of the thin end.

14

Continue, marking along the length of the legs.

15

16

To mark the face, use the Dresden tool, starting mid-forehead and using fine, short, and shallow strokes. Then mark the nose outline, nostrils, and mouth.

To mark the toes, use the thin end of a Dresden tool. Then, to mark the claws, indent with the fat end of the tool.

17

Using a fine paintbrush and edible black paint, make large black pupils. The nose, mouth, insides of the ears, and claws can be marked out with the same colour.

Tip!

For a more realistic look, once the painted facial features are dry, paint the eyes and nose with some confectioner's varnish.

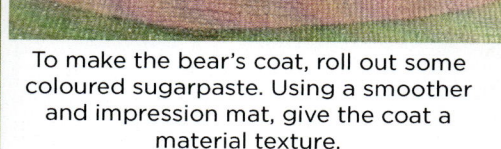

18

To make the bear's coat, roll out some coloured sugarpaste. Using a smoother and impression mat, give the coat a material texture.

Templates!

Using the templates at the end of this tutorial and your coloured sugarpaste that you texturised in the previous step, cut out the jacket.

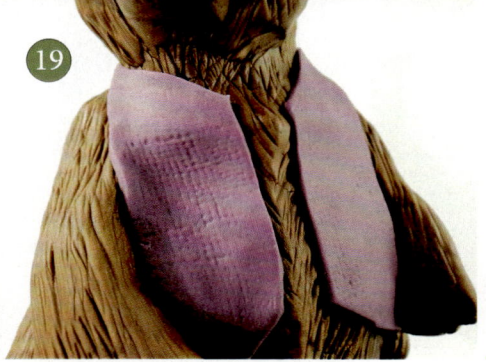

19 Attach the jacket's main back and 2 front panels with a little water.

20 Add the collars along the inside edge of the jacket and up around the neck.

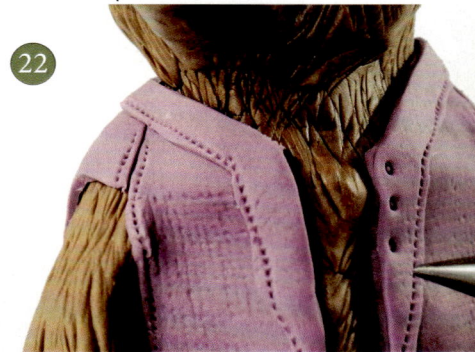

22 Using a size 1 piping nozzle, mark the buttonholes.

21 Using a stitching wheel tool, add stitching to anywhere that the fabric would normally have a seam.

23 To create the cane, roll a thin sausage of black sugarpaste. Push a 7cm-long piece of florist's wire into the sausage and roll to cover the wire. Add a small ball to the top.

24 Roll a small amount of black sugarpaste. Using 6cm- and 4cm-diameter circle cutters, cut out a donut shape.

25 Place it onto the head, letting it flop naturally.

26 Roll 50g of black sugarpaste into a barrel shape, 5cm wide and 3cm tall. Indent the top for character. Place it on top of the head.

27 Using your smallest flower cutter, make a tiny flower. Attach it to 3cm of slightly curved florist wire. Stick the wire to the front left of the hat, as in the picture. Add some tiny leaves and a 3mm-wide strip of red sugarpaste ribbon.

28 To decorate the top of the cake board, cover it with a lumpy piece of green sugarpaste. To mark some grass, push a pot brush or nail brush into the paste. Trim the edges.

29 To make the cobblestones of a forest path, take some light grey and some black sugarpaste. Mix them together, stopping while it still looks marbled.

(30)

(31)

Break off pea-sized pieces 1 at a time, taking from different sides to ensure variance in the pattern. Push each piece onto the grass. The path looks best if there's a variety of shapes and sizes.

Add some flower-shaped sprinkles.

Made with my *bear* hands.

PRODUCTS USED IN THIS TUTORIAL

Select Ireland Supreme Sugarpaste

Vera Miklas™ Modelling Chocolate

BEAR JACKET
TEMPLATES

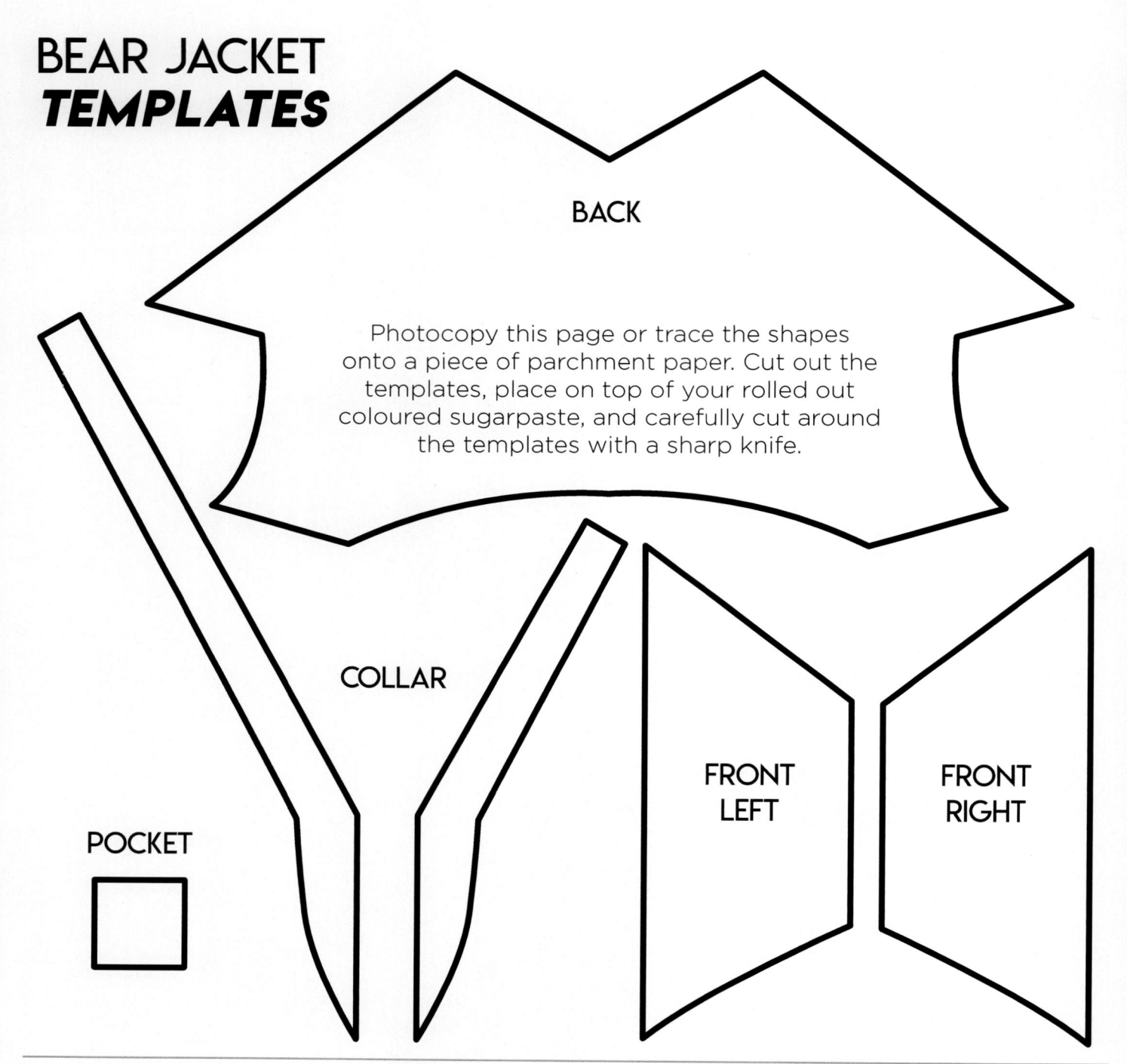

BACK

Photocopy this page or trace the shapes onto a piece of parchment paper. Cut out the templates, place on top of your rolled out coloured sugarpaste, and carefully cut around the templates with a sharp knife.

COLLAR

FRONT LEFT

FRONT RIGHT

POCKET

Paul Redmond — www.facebook.com/purplefeathercakedesign

"I can resist everything except temptation."
Oscar Wilde

INTERMEDIATE
TUTORIALS

Phoenix Park, Dublin
Photograph by Max Geraghty

Karen Geraghty

Bake Cake Create — Dublin

Hi, I'm Karen! I'm originally from Belfast, Northern Ireland, but I now live in Dublin. I moved to Dublin in 1998—without hesitation—following my one true love, a Limerick man (now my husband) whom I met in Queen's University in Belfast. After we married in 2000, we moved to Paris, France, for six years. What an eye opener in terms of fantastic cuisine and fine pastries and cakes!

While I always loved to cook and catered many a dinner party, I fell into cake decorating by accident when a friend asked me to make and decorate a Christmas cake about six years ago.

Oh, how proud I was of those lopsided penguins and that dodgy-looking igloo.

When my first son was born, I gave up my busy career as a manager in pharmaceutical clinical trials. I had spent years at university, gaining a Psychology degree, a Masters degree in Computer Science, and, finally, a PhD in Therapeutics and Pharmacology, but I was happy to give it all up to be a stay-at-home mum. When my second son was of school age, I decided that I needed to do something to occupy myself. I felt that I needed to veer towards doing something creative because I've always been creative, and it still allowed me to have time with my family. I already had a good understanding of baking because my mum had me helping her in the kitchen from a young age, making cakes. I still enjoy baking, but it's decorating that I love most, turning a blank canvas into something very special.

I am self-taught, and I spent lots of time watching tutorials and practising until I felt I was good enough to start up my business, Bake Cake Create. I have had such great experiences in this career: winning awards for my cakes, making lifelong cake friends, and creating the craziest cakes ever.

HULA HOOP
GIRL FIGURE
by Karen Geraghty

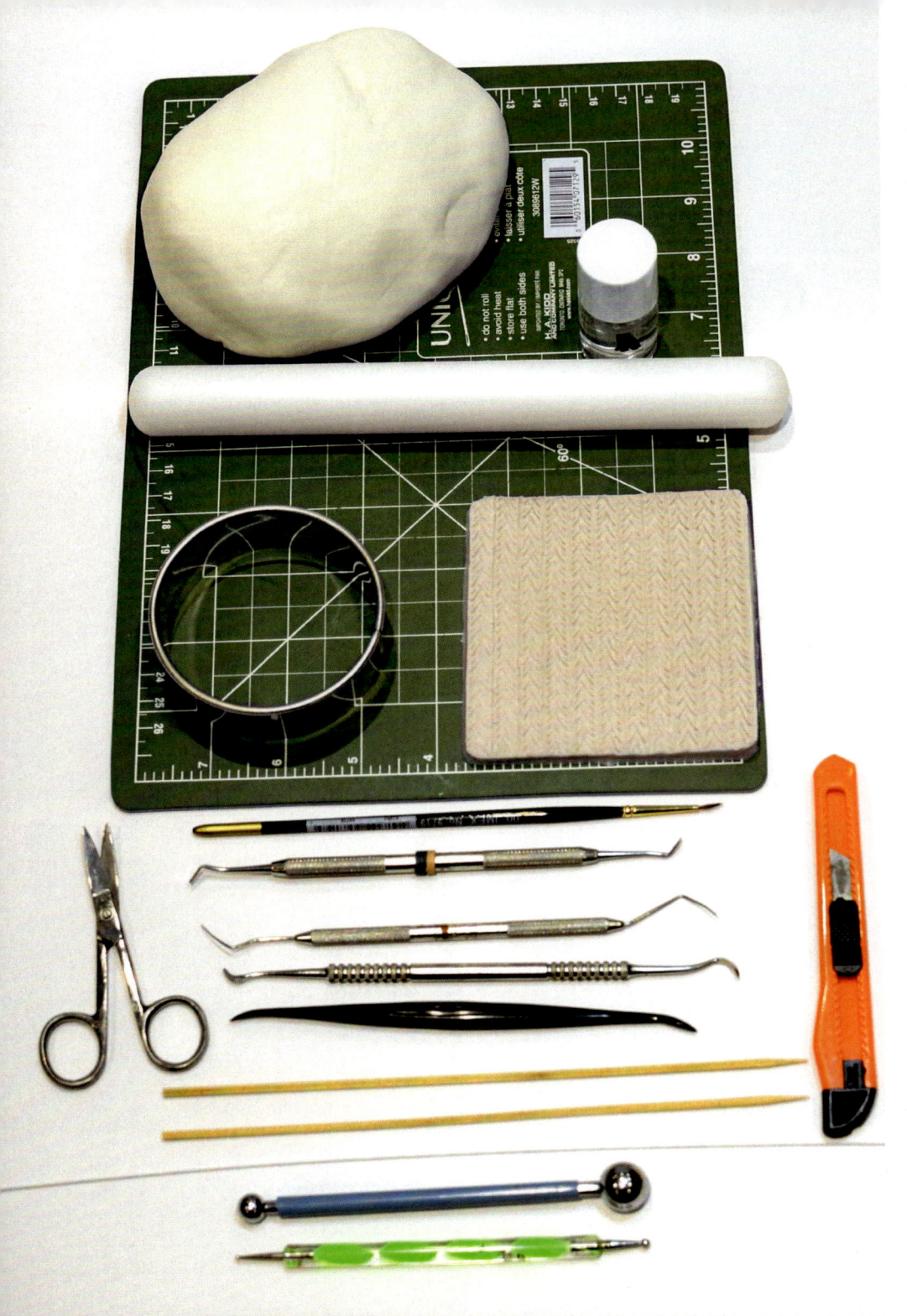

A lot of people struggle with model making, so I hope that this tutorial breaks it down and helps you with your sugar models. The weights of modelling paste will vary, as you may want to increase or decrease the size of your model according to the cake or dummy on which it stands.

A rule of thumb for height measurements for children of this age (approximately six to eight years old) is that their total height should be about four to five heads high.

EQUIPMENT AND SUPPLIES

	Modelling paste
	(Saracino)
55g/2oz	*Flesh colour*
	(head, torso, arms)
30g/1oz	*Blue colour (legs)*
10g/.35oz	*Beige colour (boots)*
15g/.5oz	*Pink colour (cardigan)*
10g/.35oz	*Yellow colour (hair)*
	Modelling chocolate
	Rolling pin
	Mat
	Scalpel/X-Acto® knife
	Wooden skewers
	and cocktail sticks
	Ball tools
	Modelling tools
	Knitting mould
	Paintbrush
	Scissors
	Dresden tool
	Stitching tool
	Florist wire
	Metal ring cutter
	Pastes to colour sugarpaste
	Dusts for jeans and face
	Water/edible glue
	Icing tip

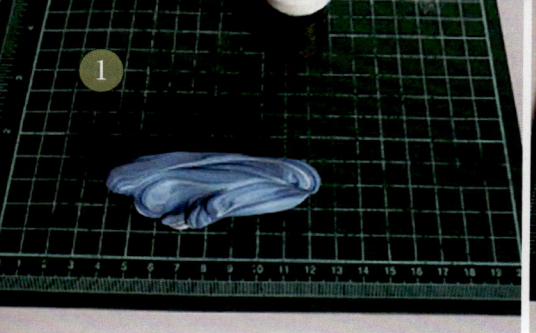

To make the blue jeans, colour your modelling paste with royal blue but don't completely mix it in. We're aiming for a faded jeans look, so keep it marbled.

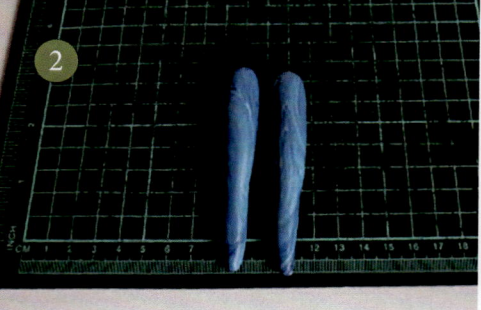

Roll 2 sausages for legs, tapering them in at 1 end.

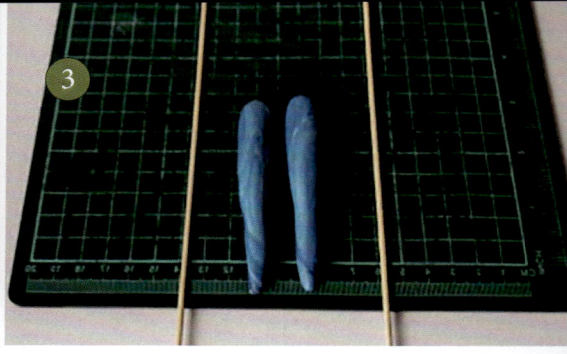

To support the leg structure and torso, insert a wooden skewer into each 'leg'. The skewers will also insert the model into your cake for stability.

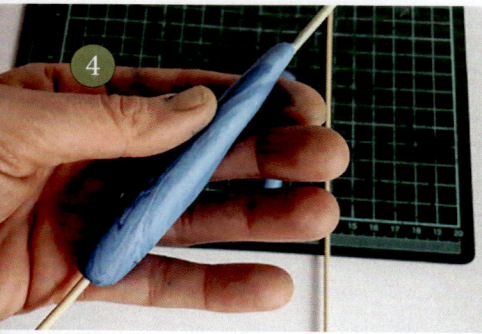

Lightly wet the skewers in water and shake off any excess. Gently twist the skewers into the legs. Don't be tempted to push them in because the leg shape will become distorted.

To make the backs of the knees, place each leg on your mat and, with the edge of your pinkie finger, gently roll the paste back and forth.

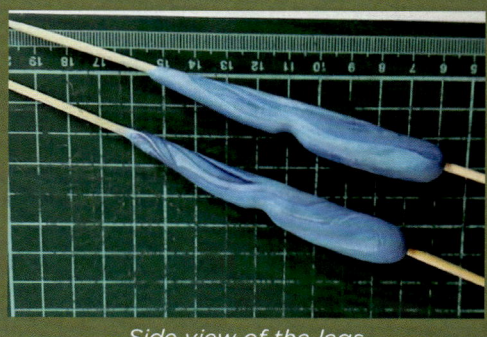

Side view of the legs showing the indentations for the backs of the knees

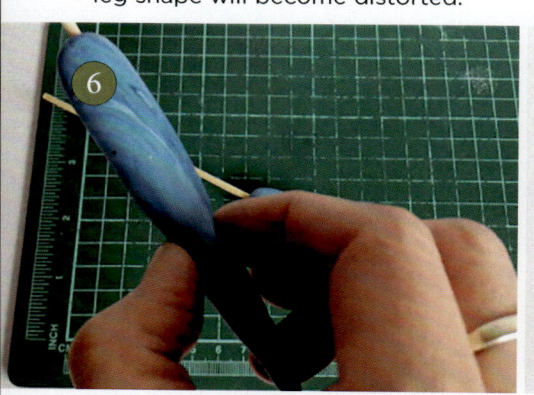

To begin forming the fronts of the knees, at the front of each leg, gently pinch in at the sides.

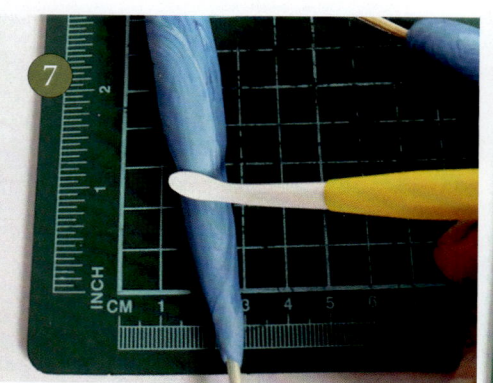

To form the undersides of the knees, use the Dresden tool to gently push the paste in a semi-circular movement from left to right.

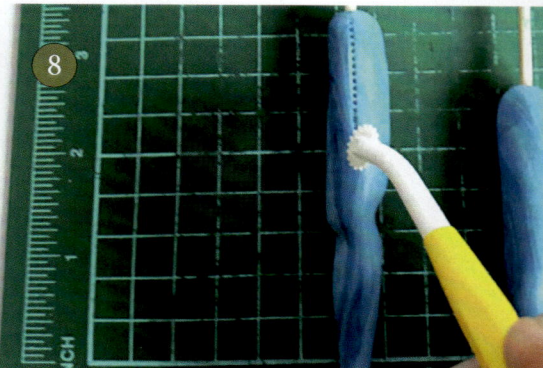

Use a stitching tool on the outside and inner side of each leg.

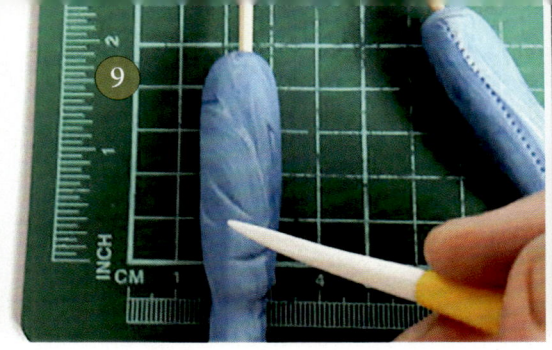

To give the jeans a wrinkled, creased look, use your Dresden tool to mark creases into each leg.

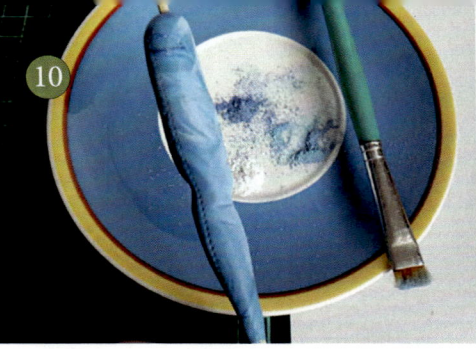

I like to use a variety of dusts to help achieve the faded jeans look; dust directly onto the legs with a suitable dry paintbrush.

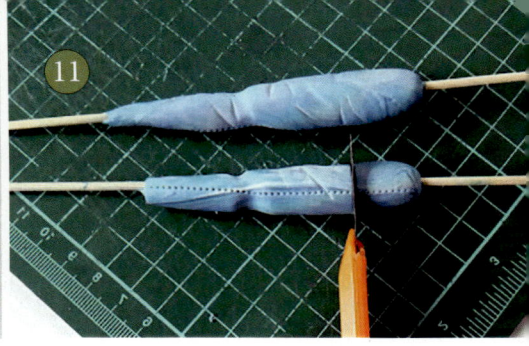

The legs may need to be shortened according to the size of the model. Use your scalpel to cut neatly.

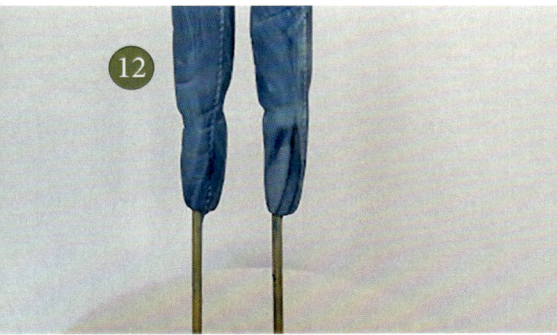

Place the legs into a dummy and allow to dry.

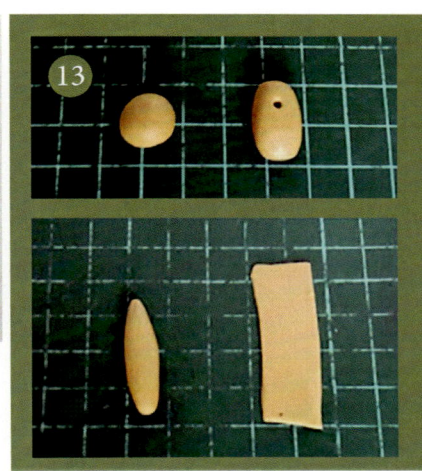

Start to prepare the boots for your model. I used a chestnut-coloured paste. Roll 2 small balls of modelling paste into a little sausage. These balls will be the 'feet' of the boots. Flatten slightly. Using a wooden skewer, pierce a small hole at 1 end of each.

To make the leg surround of each boot, roll 2 skinny sausages and roll out flat.

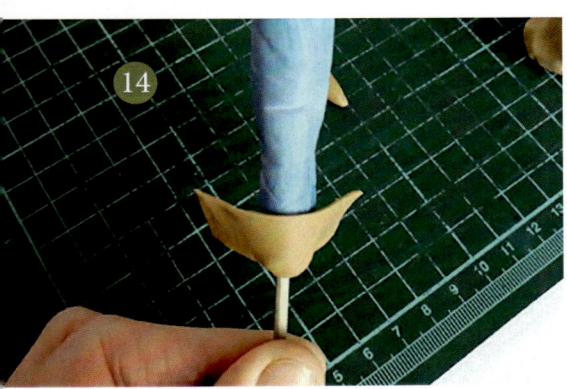

Wrap the flat leg surrounds around the bottom of each dampened leg. Leave a gap at the top of the boot so that it's not skin tight.

Add the feet to the bottom of each leg. Insert the legs into your dummy again to dry.

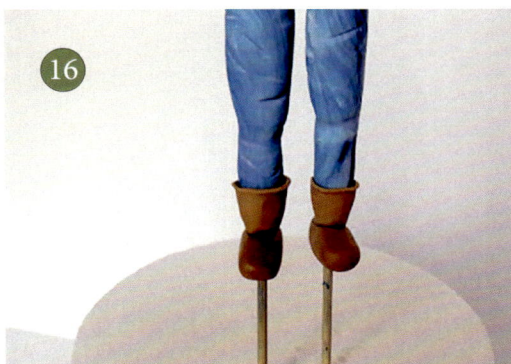

Keep the feet up off of the dummy, or they may distort and create 'cankles' if you push the skewers all the way down.

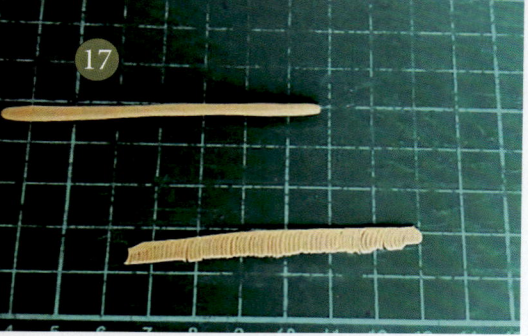

17 Roll out a long, thin sausage of modelling paste in the same colour as the boots. Cut fringes with the scalpel a couple of millimetres from the top. Repeat twice.

18 Dampen the tops of each fringe and attach to the bottoms of the legs. Attach the second fringes halfway up. Attach the third fringes just below the tops of the leg surrounds. Cut off any excess at the back.

19 To give the fringes movement, use a cocktail stick. Place them in the dummy to fully dry. Once the legs are firm, push them down so that the feet touch the dummy.

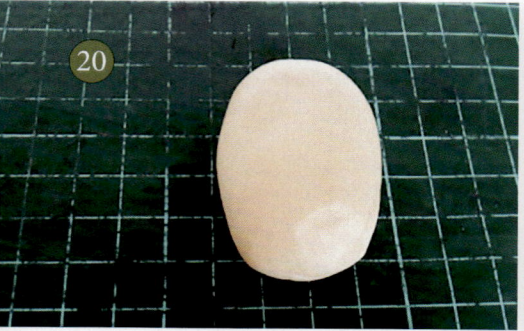

20 Colour paste with ivory, peach, or caramel until you achieve a flesh colour. Make enough paste for the model's hands, arms, and head. Shape the paste into a generic torso shape.

21 To form a neck, start to pull out the paste at the top. To form the shoulders, using your fingers only, start by pressing down from the neck and pulling out left and right, always rounding off with your fingers to create a smooth shape.

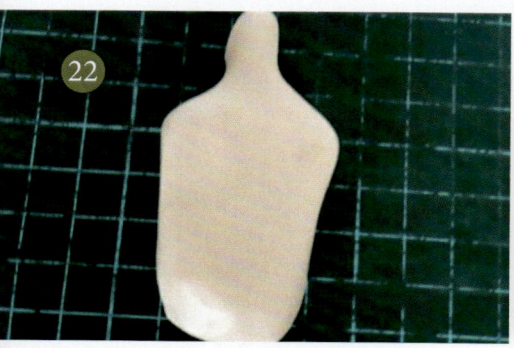

22 Continue shaping the torso and neck until you're happy with it. Cut off any excess at the bottom so that it's an appropriate size for your model's legs.

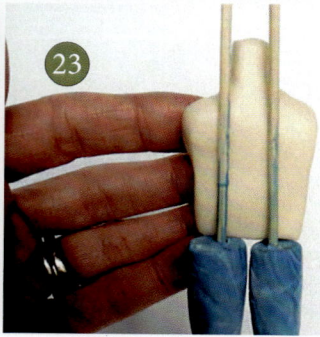

23 Ensure your torso is the right size by holding it up against your model. The neck and torso combined should be approximately the same length as the legs.

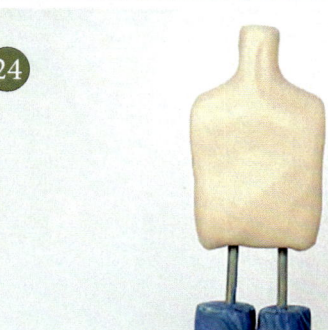

24 Cut the wooden skewers so that they're hidden inside the torso. Dampen the exposed skewers and the tops of the legs. Gently press the torso onto them.

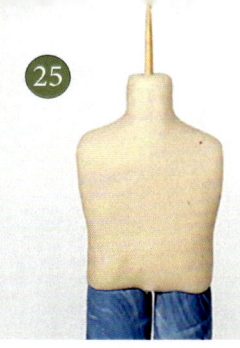

25 Once the torso is placed flush with the legs and you're happy with the shape, insert a cocktail stick into the neck. This stick will support the head.

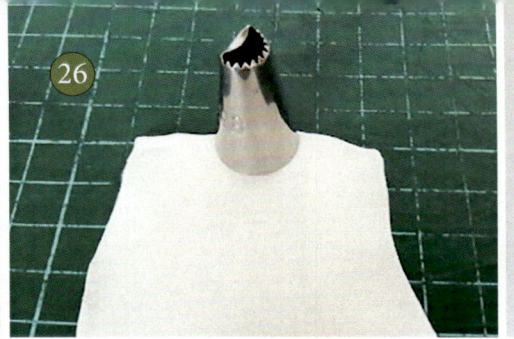

26 To prepare the T-shirt, roll out some white modelling paste. Use a circle cutter or a piping tube to cut out the area around the neck.

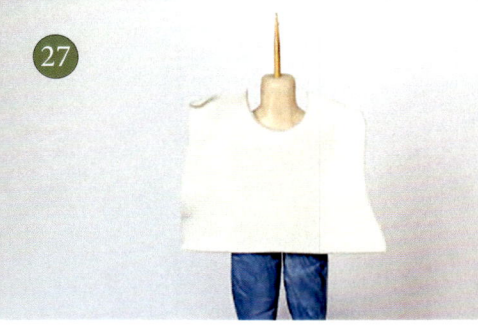

27 Slightly dampen the torso and place the T-shirt onto it. Don't worry about covering the back of the torso with the T-shirt because the cardigan will cover it.

28 Wrap the T-shirt onto the torso, cutting off any excess. Leave a little space between the T-shirt and the trousers. To create a bit of movement, add a couple of creases.

29 To prepare the cardigan, colour your paste (I used a dusky pink). Roll the paste out flat to about 2–3 mm. Use a knitting mould to create this effect.

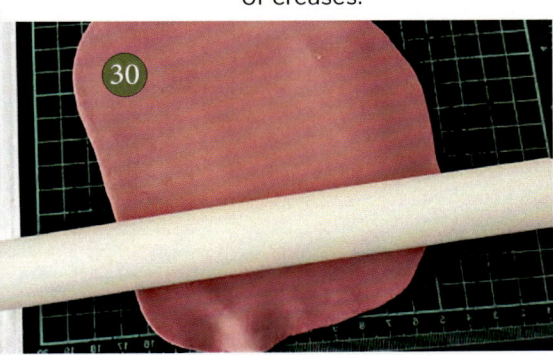

30 Place your paste over the knitting mould and firmly roll over it with your rolling pin.

31 You should have a lovely knitted effect appropriate for all types of clothing.

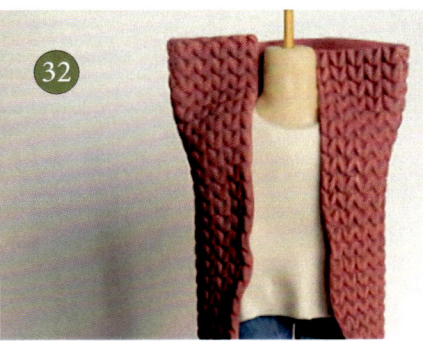

32 Cut your knitted modelling paste to the correct length and wrap it around your model. To make a good seal, tightly pinch the excess together at the tops of the shoulders.

Use scissors to cut the excess at the tops of the shoulders.

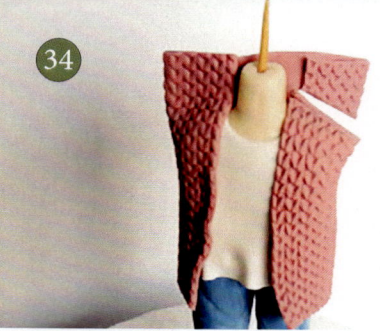

Once cut, gently smooth around the shoulders.

If you lose a little of the effect of the knitted pattern, gently press the knitting mould against the cardigan.

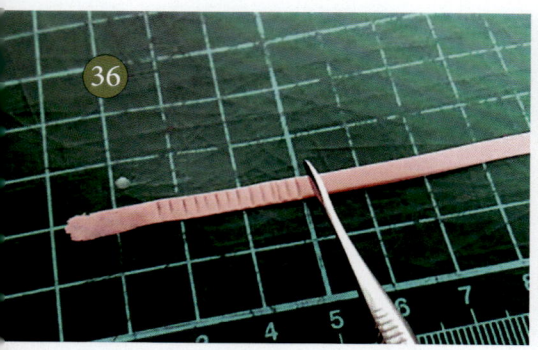

To make a ribbed effect to border the edges of the cardigan, roll out a thin, flattened sausage of modelling paste. Use a modelling tool to create the 'ribs'.

Using a little water, attach the ribbed border to the cardigan.

Roll 2 small balls of florist paste. Using edible pen or paint, paint on the irises of the eyes.

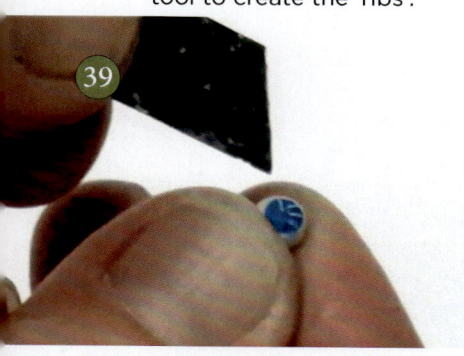

To create irises that aren't uniform in colour, use the edge of your scalpel to gently scrape lines into each iris.

Paint 2 black pupils onto the eyeballs. Add a rim to the irises using a fine paintbrush or edible pen.

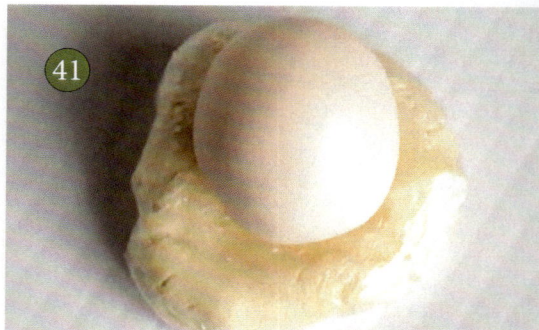

Using your flesh-coloured paste, roll a ball for the head. When working on the facial features, use a former so that the back of the head doesn't get squashed or flattened.

Check that the size of the head is appropriate for the rest of the body. The model's total height should be no more than 5 heads high for this age.

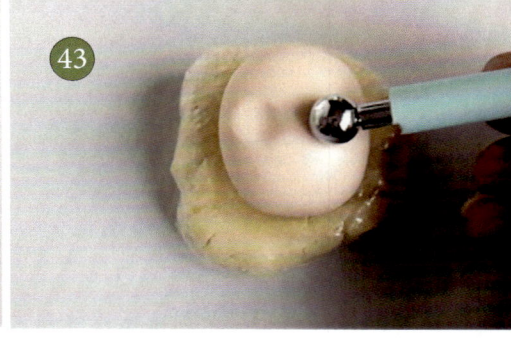

Starting with the eyes, use a ball tool to gently press into the modelling paste at the ball's centre.

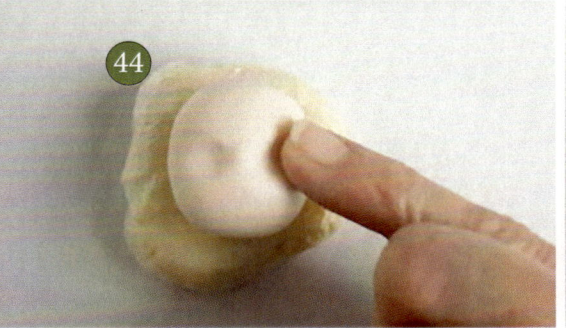

Using your little finger, gently stroke out from the indented sockets to the sides of the face.

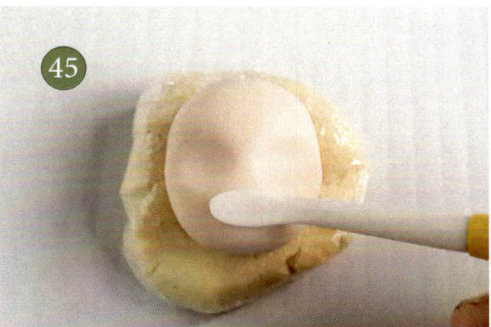

To begin shaping the nose, use the Dresden tool to gently press the modelling paste just under the eye sockets.

You can see the basic nose shape forming here.

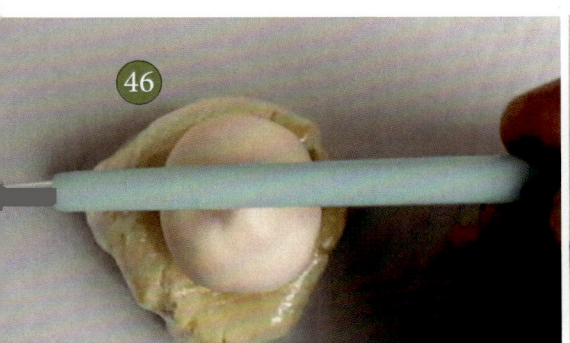

To make the nose smaller and more childlike, gently press the length of your ball tool midway between the bottom of the nose and the tops of the eye sockets.

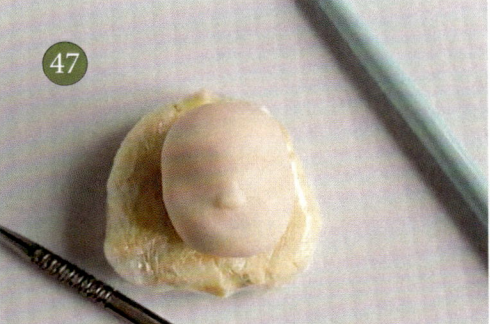

The nose should resemble a little mosquito bite. Shape the nose with your tools until you're satisfied that it's proportional for a child's face

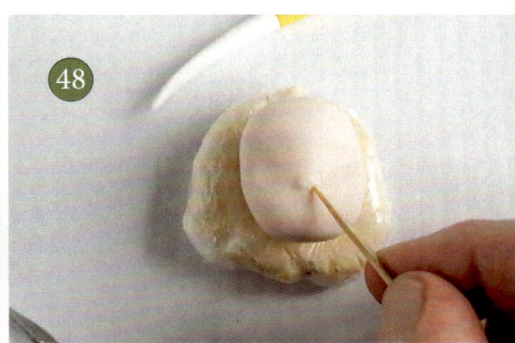

Using the end of a cocktail stick, form the nostrils.

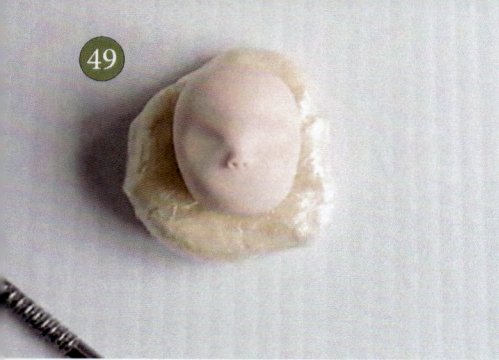

49 Ensure the eye sockets are still visible. Use your ball tool again if required. Using modelling tools, continue shaping the nose.

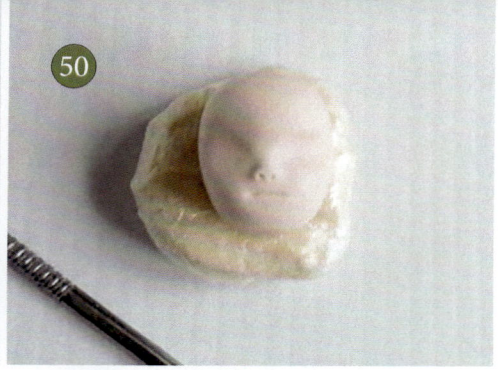

50 For the mouth, using your scalpel, cut a horizontal line just under the nose.

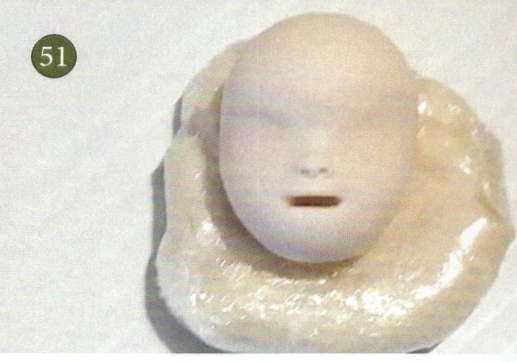

51 To open up the mouth, insert your Dresden tool flat side upwards, curved side downwards into the line.

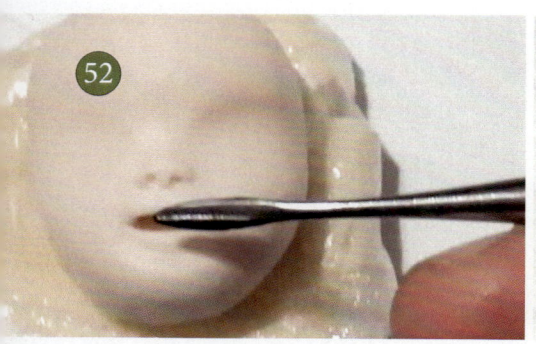

52 Insert the Dresden tool flat side up against the upper lip and pull the upper lip out from the face. Pull the modelling paste out and slightly upwards.

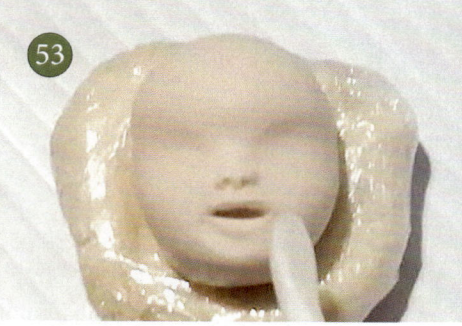

53 To form the upper lip, using the Dresden tool, starting at the centre of the upper lip, gently press upwards on the modelling paste (like applying lipstick). Use your own lips as a guide!

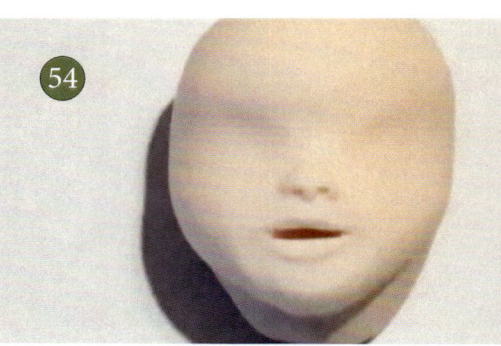

54 If the area from the mouth to chin is a little large, reshape the face by gently pressing the modelling paste downwards towards the mouth. Be careful not to distort the chin area.

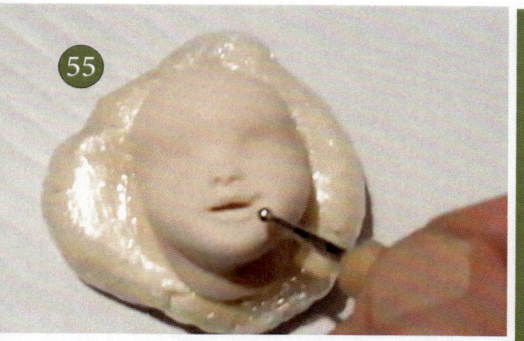

55 To form a little smile, use a small ball tool to gently press at each side of the mouth.

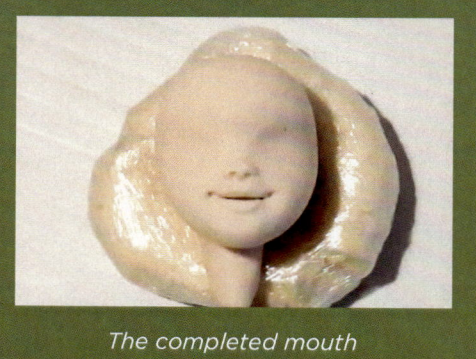

The completed mouth

56 Check your model's face from a front view and a side view to ensure the proportions are realistic.

57

Using a scalpel, mark where you want to place the eyeballs. A child's eyes are usually halfway down the face. For an adult, the eyes are placed higher.

58

Using a ball tool, indent holes big enough to fit your eyeballs. Place the eyeballs into the sockets and, using the back of your Dresden tool, gently press down.

59

Implant the eyeballs deep enough so that they don't bulge. Using the Dresden tool, smooth the modelling paste around the edge of the eyeball.

60

To line the sockets and form the part under the eyebrows, use the curved side of the Dresden tool to mark a semi-circular line above each eye.

61

Using the Dresden tool, lightly mark a line from the edge of both sides of the nose to the corner of the mouth. The older the model, the deeper the lines.

62

philtrum

To make the philtrum (the depression between the nose and the upper lip), use a ball tool.

63

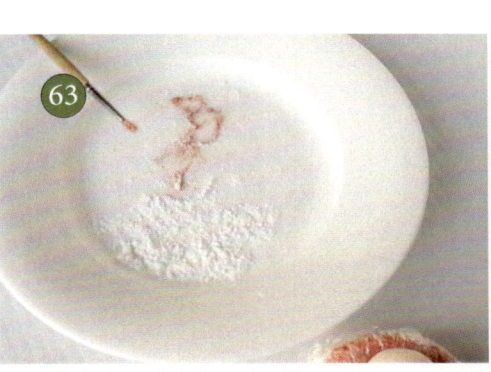

To bring the face to life, add some blush. Use a rose-coloured petal dust mixed with some corn flour so that the colour isn't too intense.

64 Mix the rose-coloured dusting powder with a little water and using a fine paintbrush, apply to the lips.

65 Using a fine paintbrush and some black paste colour, carefully paint on eyelashes.

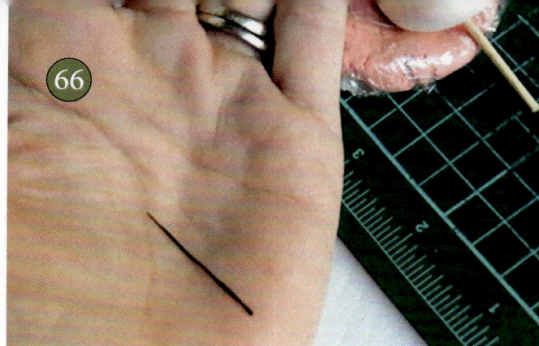

66 To apply a liner to the top of each eye, roll out some black paste in your palm, keeping it quite fine.

67 Using a fine paintbrush, dampen the edge of the top of each eye. Apply the finely rolled black paste. Use your scalpel to cut the excess at the edge of the eye.

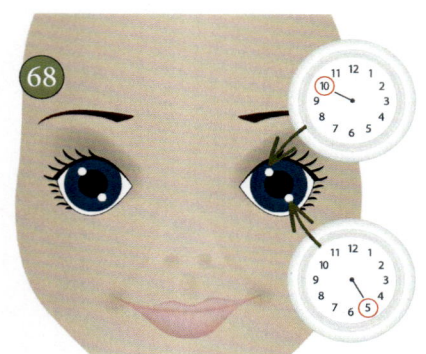

68 Glaze the iris of each eye and let dry. To create a reflection in the eyes, apply a little white spot at the 11 and 5 o'clock positions. Paint thin eyebrows above each eye.

💡 **Tip!**

If you're right-handed, paint the right eyebrow first and then turn the head upside down. This technique makes painting the left eyebrow much easier.

69 Place the head on your model to ensure dimensions, position, etc., are perfect. If the neck is too long, don't be afraid to cut it.

💡 **Tip!**

Don't stick the head on at this stage as it's easier to make the hair when the head is separate from the model.

70 Roll out a small circle of modelling paste and choose a hair colour (I chose honey gold). Dampen the head a little and then adhere the circle of paste to the top of the head.

Spread the circle of paste over the entirety of the head until it's evenly covered. Trim off any excess at the back of the head.

Using the sharp edge of the Dresden tool, make a parting along the centre of the hair. Score each side of the head to make the hair more realistic.

Roll 2 small oblongs of flesh-coloured paste for the ears. Attach them to the sides of the head with a little water. Use a small ball tool to indent and shape them.

Stick the head to the neck with a little water. Insert 2 small lengths of florist wire to support the ponytails.

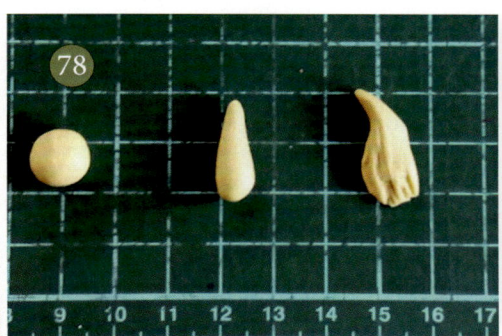

For the ponytails, roll out 2 small balls. Roll them into a teardrop shape and score with the Dresden tool. Attach to the florist wires.

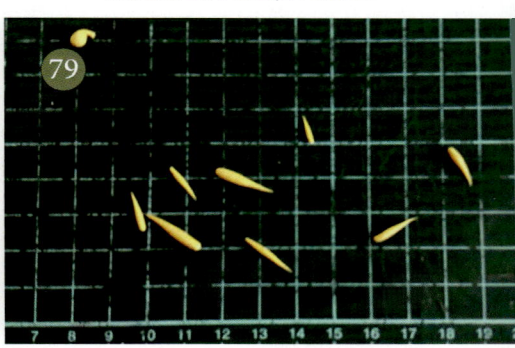

Make separate strands of hair and attach them to the front of the head at the hairline.

Attach to the ponytails with some water.

To make bows at the sides of the ponytails, make 4 small triangles, 2 triangles on each side.

Attach the bows to the tops of the ponytails with some water.

83 To make the hula hoop, use a circle cutter to make sure it fits over your model. Wrap a length of florist wire around the cutter and twist the ends to form a full circle.

84 Remove the wire from the circle cutter and cut off any excess.

85 Cover the circle of wire with neon yellow modelling chocolate. Roll out a long narrow sausage and then cut a slit along its length halfway through.

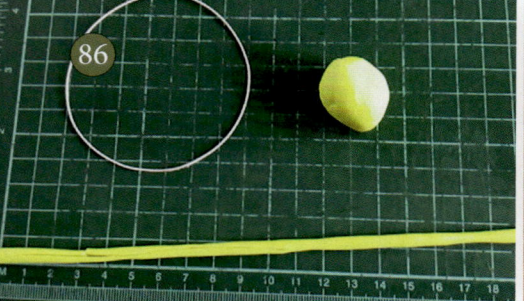

86 Use the heat of your fingers to mould the modelling chocolate around the wire circle. Use your scalpel and the warmth of your fingers to soften any sharp edges after cutting. Leave to harden.

87 Roll out the flesh-coloured paste into 2 sausages, slightly tapering 1 end. Check the length by holding them next to your model. Take into account that the arm will lengthen when you create the wrist.

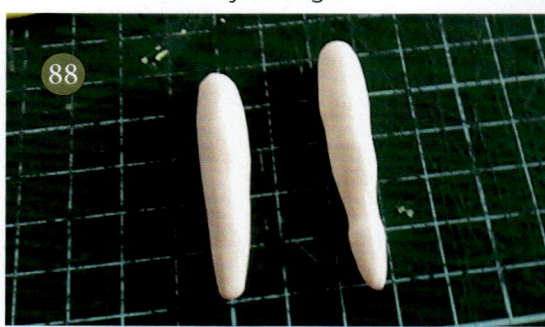

88 Using your forefingers to gently roll the modelling paste, narrow each arm at 1 end at the location of the wrist.

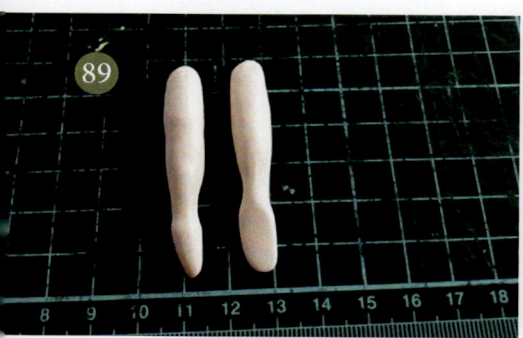

89 Flatten the area under the wrist with your forefinger.

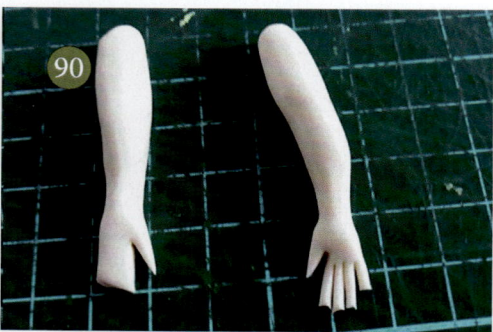

90 Cut out a section to create the thumb. Using your scalpel, split the remainder into 4 fingers. Shorten the length of the shorter fingers such as the pinkie.

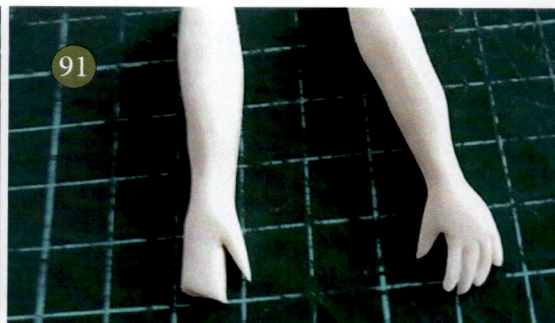

91 Gently round off the top of each finger with your own fingers by gently twisting and stroking.

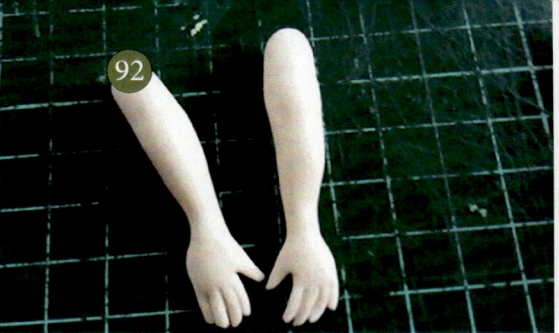

92

With the palm facing upwards, cradle in your own palm and use the rounded end of the Dresden tool to push down slightly, moving from the fingers back to the wrist.

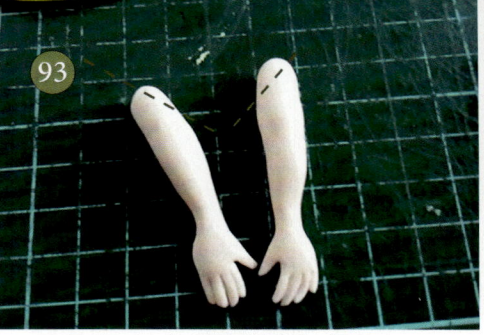

93

Using a sharp scalpel, slice the upper part of each arm at an angle so that they don't appear bulky and oversized.

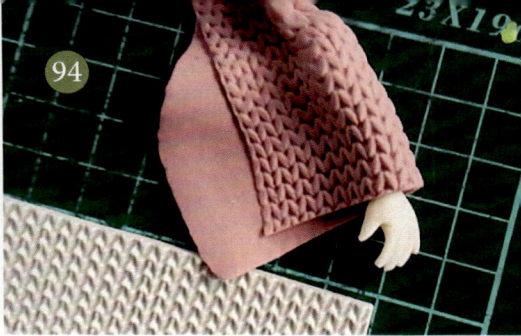

94

Using the knitting mould again, create sleeves for the arms. Attach 1 arm to the torso using water or edible glue.

95

While supporting the left side of the hula hoop with something of the right height (salt cellar in my case!), attach the other side of the hula hoop to the model's hand. Use 'gloop' to adhere instead of water for a strong hold.

(Gloop = modelling paste mixed with a little water to make a thick paste.) Shape the fingers around the hula hoop to get a tight fit.

96

Attach the other arm and follow the instructions above to fit the hand to the hula hoop. Keep the support in place until the position is held firm. Leave for a couple of hours to be sure it's secure.

97

Cover your cake with green sugarpaste. To make the covering look like grass, use a nailbrush to push into the sugarpaste. Airbrush if you want to break up the uniformity of colour. Add pretty little flowers and blades of grass. Mark out where you're going to place the model and make holes for insertion. Insert your finished model when firm. If you want, make a little scarf using the same knitting mould as before.

The Royal Hospital Kilmainham, Dublin
Photograph by Niamh Ní Riain

Gail PORTER

LizzieMay's — Kilmainham, Dublin

I fell into the wonderful world of sugarcraft back in 2012. In 2000, I finished my Business and Languages degree in Birmingham and worked in Dublin, Northampton (UK), and Galway over the next nine years. In 2009, I moved to Cork to spend 12 incredible weeks at Ballymaloe Cookery School. After the cookery course, I moved back to Galway—despite the rain, I love Ireland's stunning west coast!—and worked as a chef for the next couple of years. I knew then that my long love of baking had to be the starting point for my own business. In 2012, I left chef work and took up part-time office work to give myself time to set up LizzieMay's (named after my grannies, Lizzie and May).

I never dreamt I'd have any patience for sugarcraft, but after doing a half-day course to learn the basics of covering a cake, I was intrigued. Once I started playing with royal icing, I was properly hooked. Decorating cookies became my specialty—anything can be cookie-fied!

I moved to Dublin two years ago to live with my partner, and while my heart lies in the west, Dublin is an interesting, vibrant city. I no longer take orders, but I like to keep my hand in. I've been lucky enough to be invited to take part in some fabulous Irish collaborations, have entered a few competitions, and still run the occasional cookie decorating class.

POP ART

COOKIE POPS

by Gail Porter

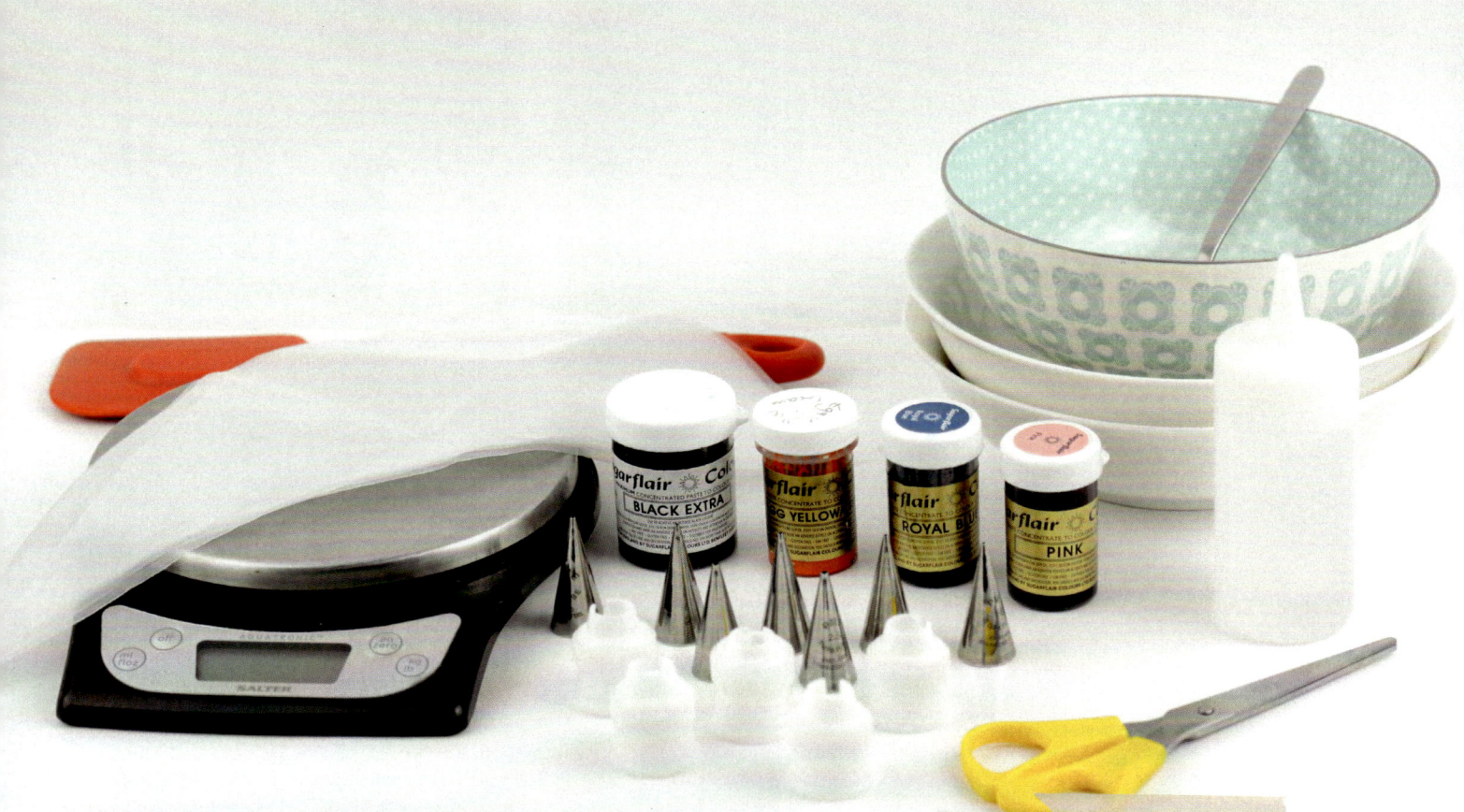

EQUIPMENT AND SUPPLIES

Baking trays
Rolling pin
Cookie cutters
Parchment paper
Cookies baked onto lollipop sticks

Royal icing
Weighing scales
Stand mixer
Spatula *(Zeal)*
2x Small bowls
Teaspoon
Squeeze bottle with water
Cling film *(plastic wrap), ideally a long, catering-style roll*
Scribe tool
6x Disposable piping bags

Scissors
6x Couplers
Edible pen
5x 1.5 PME piping tips
2x 2.5 PME piping tips
Flat paintbrush
Damp cloth
Kitchen roll
Fan *(optional)*

EDIBLE COLOURS
I used the following Sugarflair paste colours:
Black Extra
Egg Yellow
Pink
Royal Blue

A note from Gail...

Cookie decorating is all in the planning! First, think about the designs you're making and then work out the colours and consistencies you need.

When you're ready to decorate, consider designs where sections need to dry before you add further detail and plan out the order in which you decorate based on that.

1

Make royal icing, mixing until it reaches the correct consistency
(pull out some icing; the peak will just fall over but will hold that form).

2

Weigh out approximately 30g of icing
into a small bowl.

3

Press cling film onto the surface of
the remaining icing in the bowl
to prevent it crusting over.

4

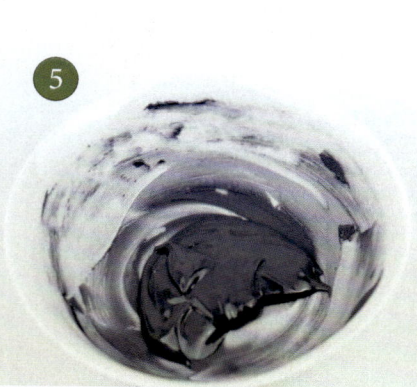

Add some black colour to the icing
using the end of a teaspoon and use
the spatula to mix it in thoroughly.

5

Use enough colour to mix to a
dark grey colour; it will develop
into black by the time you start
decorating.

6

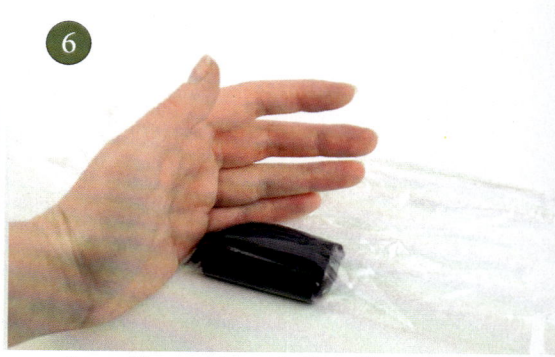

Tear off a section of cling film, pile
the icing into the centre, fold over
the film, and seal and shape with
your hand.

7

8

Roll up the icing in the cling film and pinch the ends.

9

Roll up the icing in the cling film. This packaging method allows you to pop the wrapped package into the piping bag later and minimises washing-up time when you finish decorating.

Spin it, moving your hands out to the ends as you go (try not to pull taut; think skipping rope!).

10

11

12

Weigh out 100g of icing and add yellow colour. This is more than you'll need for this set, but it'll allow for practise on any spare cookies!

Add water to create a looser, 'flooding' consistency. Add approx. 1 tsp water to start and then add a few drops at a time until it's done.

When a trail in the icing disappears after a slow count to 4, you're done.

Tip!

Don't worry if your icing is slightly thicker or thinner. Very thin icing will overflow your borders, but you have some leeway. With practise, you'll find the consistencies that are perfect for you!

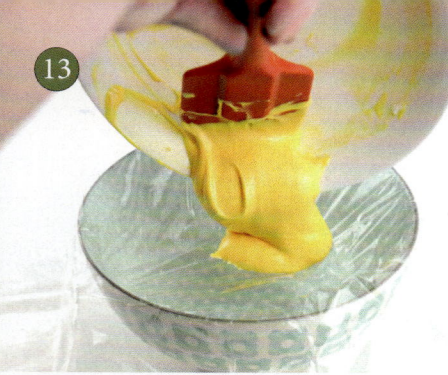

To wrap the flood icing, lay the cling film over a bowl, allow a slight dip in the middle, and then scoop the icing into the centre.

If there are large bubbles, lay the scribe tool as flat as possible across the bubble and lift straight up to pop them.

Pull up the cling film so that the icing is at the edge of the bowl.

Don't delay: pull the side of the cling film nearest you up and over the icing to contain it.

Avoid scrunching up the cling film as you lift up the package and place it on your work surface.

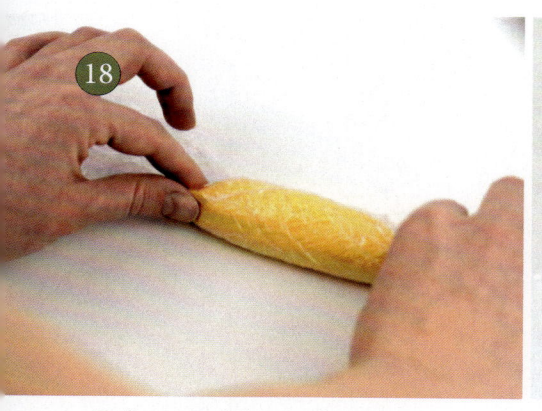

Roll up the icing in the cling film as previously and carefully spin to secure it.

Repeat steps 10–18 with each of the other colours (white, pink, and blue) and gather your piping bags and couplers.

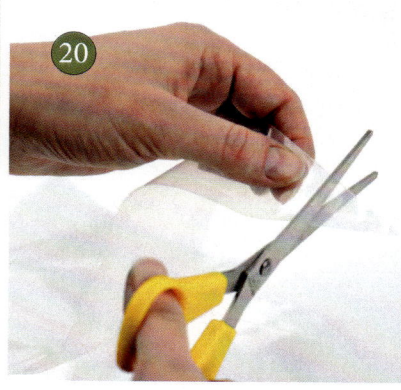

Cut off a small piece from the end of one of the piping bags.

21 Unscrew a coupler and drop the larger piece into the bag. The hole in the bag should come to the top of the coupler (the bag will cover the 'screw' section).

22 Repeat with the remaining bags. Carefully line them up with the first bag to mark exactly how much to cut off.

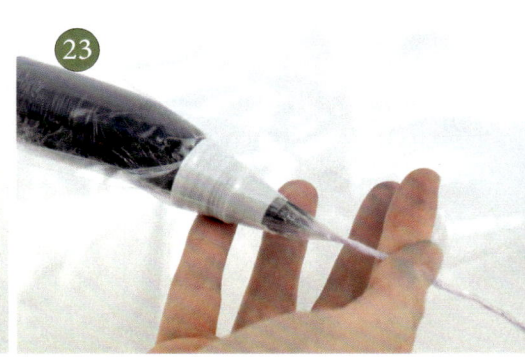

23 Feed the packaged icing into the bags and use the spun cling film to pull through until the icing can be seen at the top of the coupler.

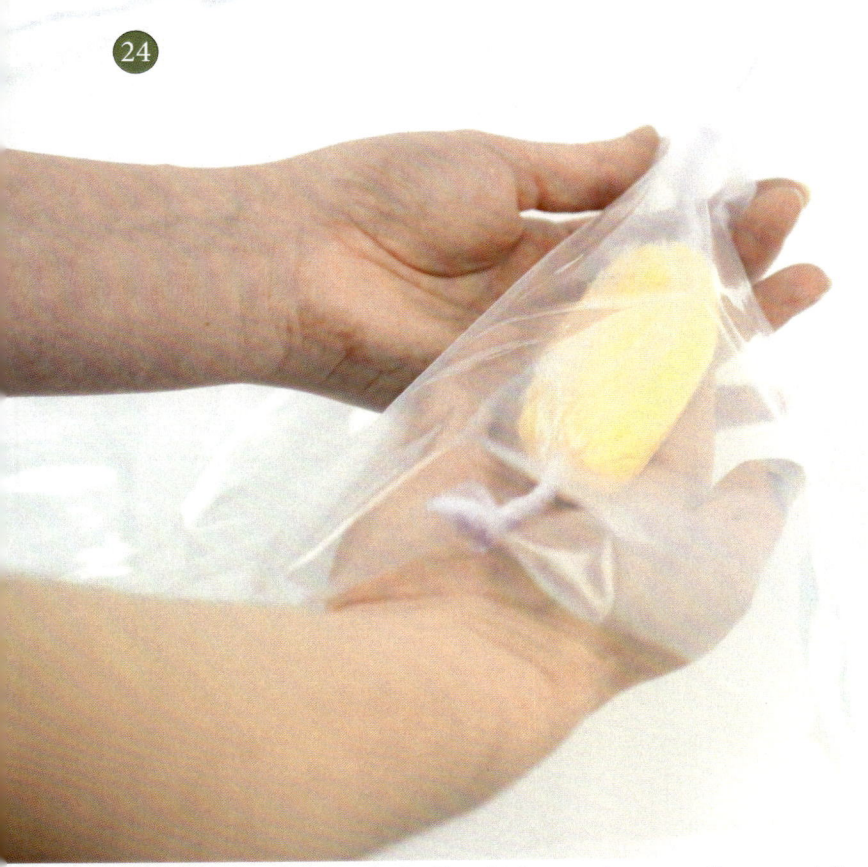

24 Take particular care with the flood icing packages as they are delicate. Feed them through in the palm of your hand rather than drop them in.

25 Finally! Use an edible marker to mark out the patterns on the flower, star, mask, and lips cookies.

WOW!

Get your Wow! template ready from page 84 at the end of this tutorial. Print or redraw the template, place on a board, and tape a piece of acetate over the top, ensuring everything is completely flat and secure. Make more than one Wow! transfer in case one breaks.

Icing ready!

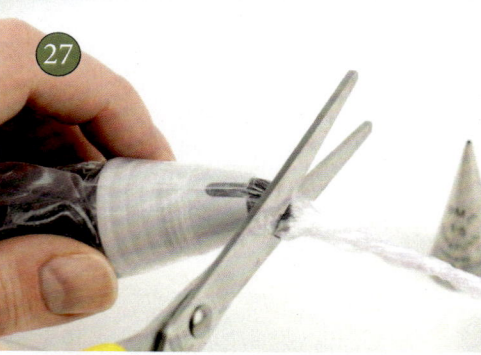

Take your bag of black icing and cut off the end of the cling film.

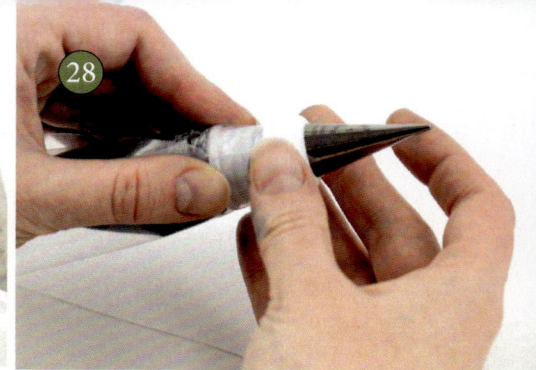

Put on a 1.5 tip and secure with the other part of the coupler.

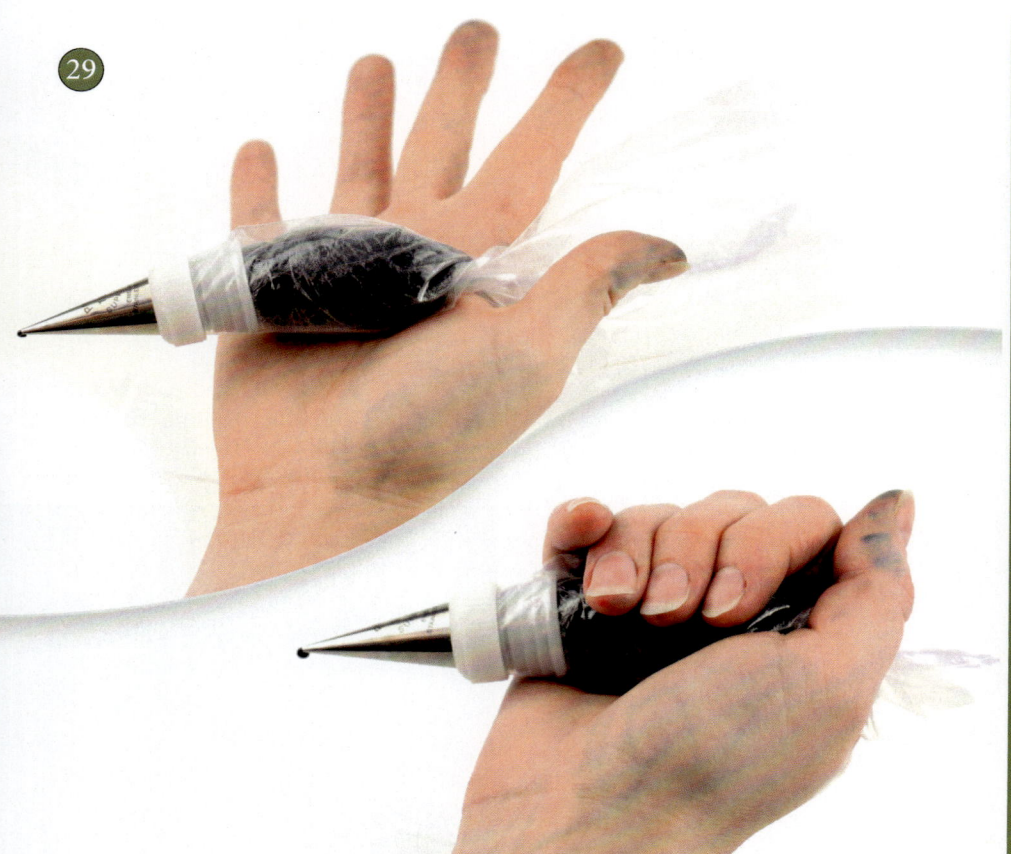

Twist the top of the bag and hold the twist between your thumb and forefinger so that the icing sits in the palm of your hand. This technique may feel awkward at first, but it gives me the most control and comfort.

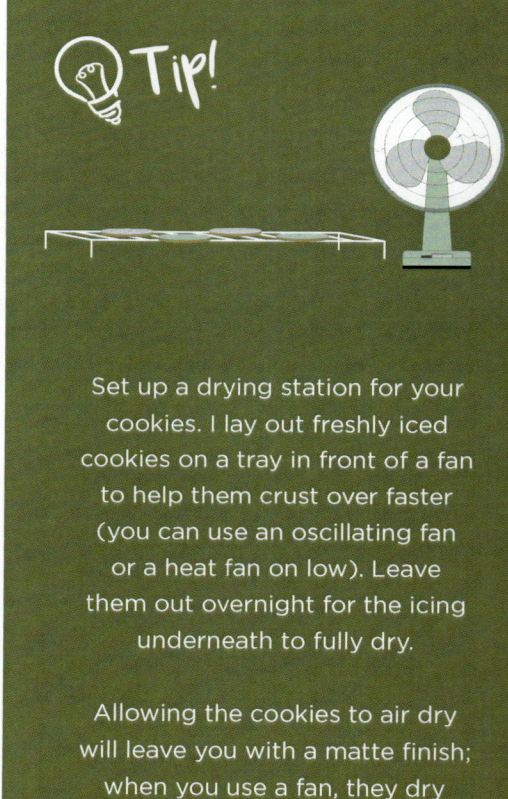

Tip!

Set up a drying station for your cookies. I lay out freshly iced cookies on a tray in front of a fan to help them crust over faster (you can use an oscillating fan or a heat fan on low). Leave them out overnight for the icing underneath to fully dry.

Allowing the cookies to air dry will leave you with a matte finish; when you use a fan, they dry with a slight sheen, which I love.

A LITTLE PRACTISE FUN!

TO PIPE DOTS

Hold the piping bag vertically and position the tip barely above the surface. Squeeze, stop squeezing, and then gently lift away.

TO PIPE LINES

Hold the piping bag at a 45° angle and position the tip barely above the surface at your starting point. Start squeezing and pipe up and away from the surface to a height of about 1 inch and then think about it as 'laying down' the icing. Keep the pressure steady, keep the piping tip ahead of where the icing touches the surface, and keep that curve in the icing at the bottom. This technique shows that you aren't stretching or pulling the icing. When you near the end, you can judge how much icing is already piped out and lay it down until the tip is back at the surface.

Holding the tip away from the surface gives you lots of control. This technique gives you flexibility and control. Holding the tip away from the surface makes it easier to change direction at any point, and if you're unsure of where to go next, you can simply stop piping and the icing will stay in place while you figure it out.

If you're rushing to keep up with the flow of icing, ease up on the pressure. I use my right hand to control the flow of icing, with my arm against the edge of the table for stability, and I use my left hand to help control the direction of the icing and keep everything steady.

Tip! Keep the tip clean: I always have a damp cloth and a scrap piece of paper nearby so that I can pipe out a little icing to check the consistency and make sure there are no clogs before I start piping.

Time to outline! Start with your Wow! template and pipe over the outline onto the acetate.

Outline all your cookies with the black icing, including the inner drawn designs to create a barrier to hold in the flooding-consistency icing.

Turn the cookie around if needed so that you're piping in a direction that feels comfortable.

33

If you've piped a slightly wobbly line, use a barely damp brush to carefully nudge it into place.

34

35

Move your scribe tool in a circular motion to gently nudge out the icing to catch on the black outline.

Using a 1.5 tip, pipe the pink icing in the middle of the first 'W'. Pipe carefully and close to the surface, as this flood icing is a looser consistency than the black icing.

36

Flood the second 'W'. Allow it to crust over before flooding the 'O' and '!'. This technique helps avoid the letters flooding into each other.

Tip!

The most efficient way to flood a set of cookies is to pick one colour at a time and flood all the cookies in the set using that colour. Bear in mind, some sections may need to crust over before you can flood an adjacent section.

37

Using a 1.5 tip, flood the middle section of the flower with yellow icing, using your scribe tool to carefully nudge the icing to the outline. Move to your drying station.

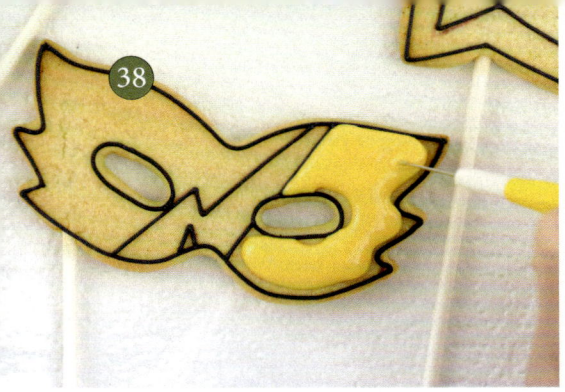

Flood the right side of the mask, using your scribe tool as before. Move to your drying station.

White next! Using a 2.5 tip, pipe icing into the centre of the cookie. Use your scribe tool to carefully nudge the icing to the outline.

The top of the lips has a wet-on-wet, polka-dot pattern. Flood the yellow base as usual and then quickly pipe a row of dots with the pink icing. Use this row as a guide to pipe the other rows of dots. As both are flood consistency, the dots sink in to the base and the pattern will dry flat. Move to your drying station.

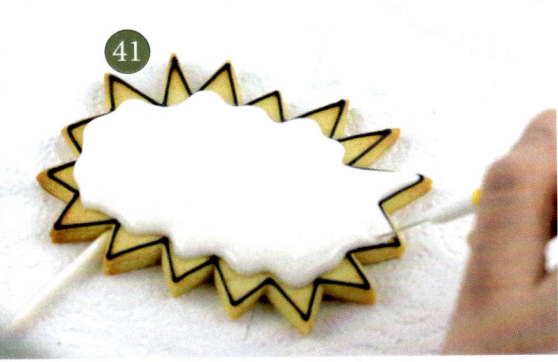

As with the lips, immediately pipe on blue polka-dots, this time with a 2.5 tip. Move the finished cookie to your drying station.

Carrying on with the blue, flood the moustache cookie. Create stripes by immediately piping rows of white and then yellow icing.

Remember that you're adding more icing each time, so be careful not to flood too heavily with the blue. Move to your drying station.

44 Flood the outside of the star cookie in blue and pipe on small dashes of white in random directions. Move to your drying station.

Tip!

Keep your paintbrush nearby. If you accidentally flood over the outline, a barely damp paintbrush can gently take away excess icing.

45 Flood the other half of the mask cookie with pink icing and move to your drying station,

46 Flood the bottom lip with pink, keeping the black centre line visible. Immediately pipe yellow polka-dots and move to your drying station.

47 Retrieve your Wow! transfer from the drying station. If using a heater fan, cool completely before proceeding.

48 Flood the remaining sections, taking particular care where the borders meet the other letters. Return to the drying station and dry overnight.

49 Retrieve your flower-shaped cookie and flood the blue section.

50 Flood the white section, taking particular care along the border with the yellow section.

51 Immediately pipe rows of small pink polka-dots. Return to your drying station.

52

Retrieve your mask-shaped cookie and carefully flood the centre section with white icing. Pipe in a row of blue stripes using a 1.5 tip.

53

If the icing slightly overflows the outline, use a barely damp fine paintbrush to rectify. Move to your drying station.

54

Retrieve your star-shaped cookie and flood the centre with white icing.

55

Immediately pipe rows of pink polka-dots.

56

Pipe yellow dots inside the pink dots. (For a quirky design, pipe these dots slightly off-centre.) Move to your drying station.

Dry overnight

Leave your cookies and transfer to dry overnight. If you live in a humid area, you might want to allow an extra few hours' drying time the following day.

57 Use a craft knife to carefully cut away the tape securing the acetate. Put the board up on a box or book to raise it a few inches.

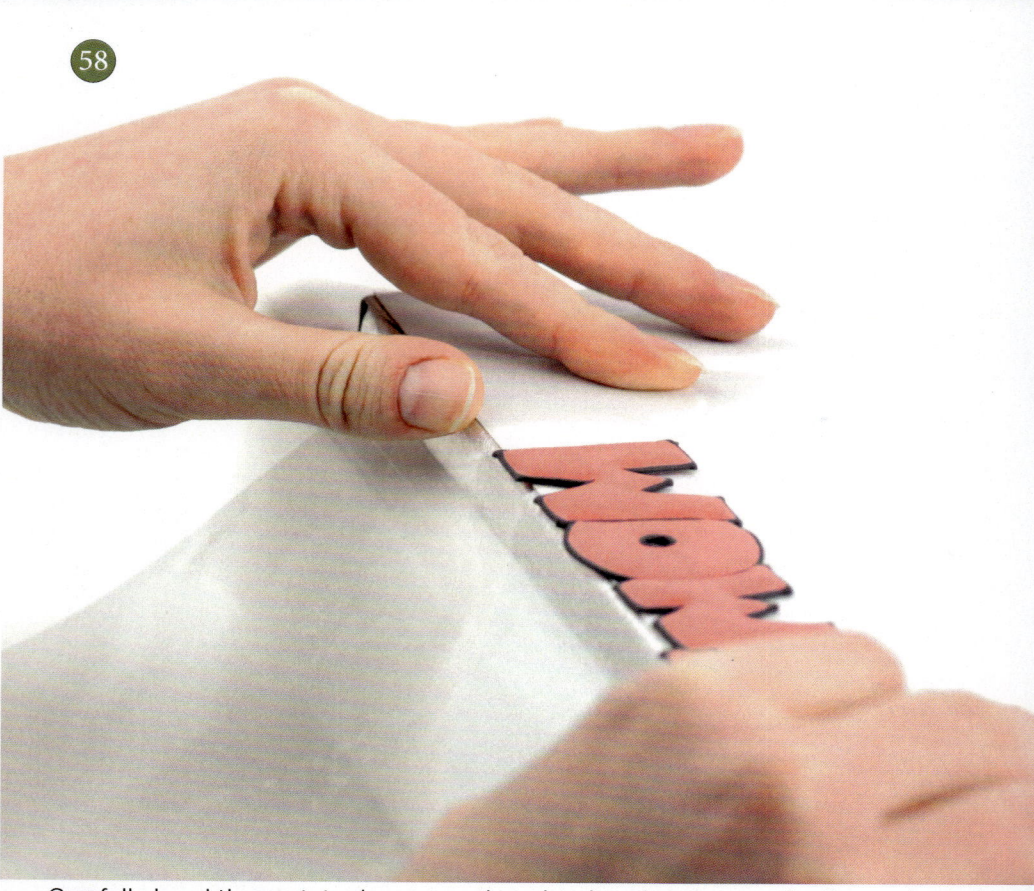

58

59 Continue to gently pull down the acetate until about half the transfer has released itself.

Carefully bend the acetate down over the edge, keeping the transfer flat on the board. Very slowly and gently pull down the acetate, and the transfer will start to release itself.

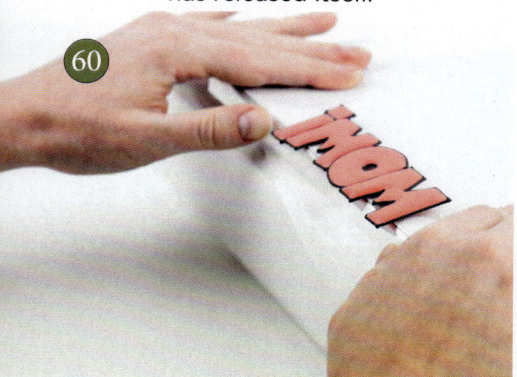

60 Turn the transfer around and carefully repeat from the other side; when you reach the middle, it will completely release itself.

61 Pipe two dots of icing onto the white and blue polka-dot cookie to secure the transfer.

62 With extreme care, peel the transfer from the acetate and lift onto the cookie, pressing down gently to stick to the base.

VANILLA COOKIES

by Gail Porter (tutorial on page 68)

Yield: 16–24 cookies
Prep time: 40 mins (plus chilling/resting time)
Baking time: 20 mins

It's important not to overwork this cookie dough. Try not to knead heavily when you're bringing it together to roll it out, cut your cookies close together, and ideally only re-roll the offcuts one more time. You'll see that any cookies rolled a third or fourth time will hold their shape better when baked, but they'll also be a little tougher!

INGREDIENTS

100g/3.5oz	Soft butter
115g/.5oz	Caster sugar
1x	Medium egg
5g/1tsp	Vanilla bean paste
	or vanilla extract
285g/10oz	Plain flour

DIRECTIONS

1. Mix together the butter, sugar, and vanilla paste or extract until smooth.

2. Add the egg in 2 parts, incorporating the first addition completely before adding the next. Scrape down the sides of the bowl if necessary.

3. Sift in the flour.

4. Gently mix until the dough just comes together. Don't worry if it's still a little crumbly!

5. On a piece of cling film, flatten out the dough to about 2cm ($^3/_4$ inch) thickness, wrap in the cling film, and refrigerate for at least an hour.

6. Preheat the oven to 180°C/350°F (160°C/325°F fan oven).

7. Line 2 cookie trays with parchment paper.

8. On a floured surface, roll out the cookie dough to about 6mm ($^1/_4$ inch) thickness.

9. Cut out a cookie shape and insert a lollipop stick. To do so, hold the stick level with your cookie and gently twist the stick back and forth, working it at least 1" into the cookie. Place your fingers flat on the top of the cookie to make sure it doesn't break through the top. If it breaks through the bottom, gently turn the cookie over and patch over the break with a small piece of dough. Turn the cookie over again and carefully place on the tray. Repeat this step with the remainder of the dough.

10. Chill or freeze the cookies for 30 minutes; they will hold their shape better during baking.

11. Bake for 10–20 minutes (depending on size); the cookies should be pale and dry to the touch.

12. The cookies will rise a little; use a fondant smoother to press down on them as soon as they're out of the oven to ensure a flat surface. Or, when you decorate, turn the cookies over and ice the flat bottom.

13. Cool on the trays for a few minutes and then move to a wire cooling rack.

14. Store in an airtight tin as soon as they're cool. They will keep well for at least 3 weeks.

ROYAL ICING

Yield: To decorate 16 - 24 cookies
Prep time: 25 mins
Drying time: Overnight

This is an old-school recipe; if you'd prefer not to use fresh egg whites, you can find cartons of pasteurised egg whites. There are many recipes online that use meringue powder or dried egg white—experiment and find the one that works for you! As a rule of thumb, I calculate how much royal icing I'll need based on 30g of icing per cookie.

INGREDIENTS

90g/3oz Egg whites
480g/17oz Icing sugar

DIRECTIONS

1. Add the icing sugar and egg whites to the bowl of your stand mixer. (I don't sieve my icing sugar.)

2. Mix on the lowest speed using the paddle attachment until the icing holds fairly stiff peaks when you lift out the beater (about 20 minutes).

3. If you're not using it straight away, press a piece of cling film directly onto the surface of the royal icing to stop it drying out.

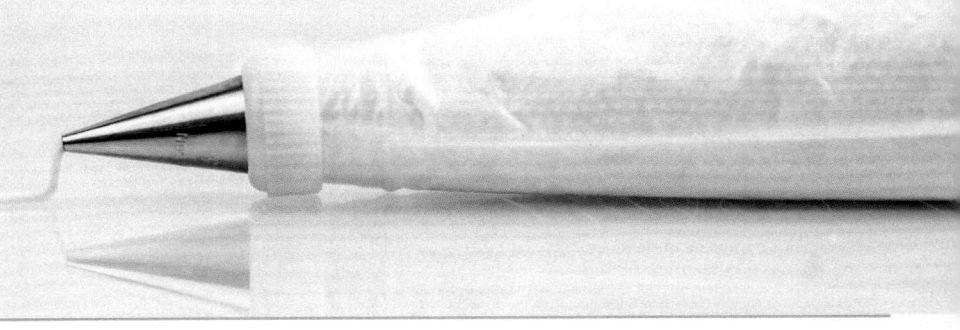

COOKIE TRACING
TEMPLATES

Gail Porter — www.facebook.com/LizzieMaysCakes

All of the techniques taught in this tutorial can be used on any cookie shape, but feel free to follow along, using these templates as a cutting guide to create the exact same cookies as Gail's.

Photocopy these pages or trace the shapes onto a piece of greaseproof paper. Cut out the templates, place on top of your rolled out cookie dough, and carefully cut around the templates with a sharp knife.

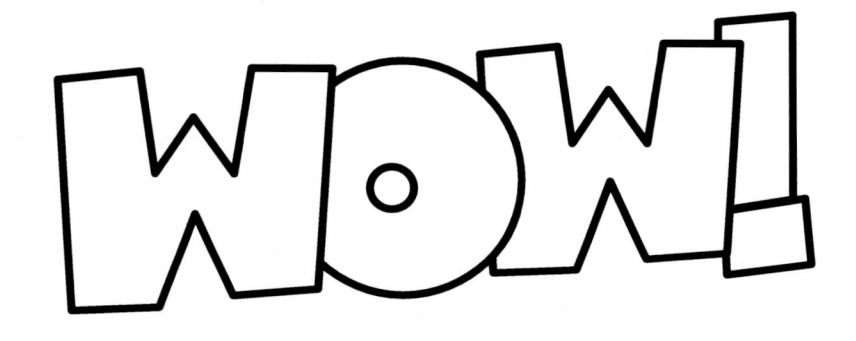

Dún na Sí, Moate, County Westmeath, Ireland
Photograph by Corinna Maguire

Tanya ROSS

Novel-T Cakes — Moate, Co. Westmeath

I was born and grew up in sunny South Africa, where I had an Industrial Engineering business. I met my husband when out on site measuring up a job—no dating apps then! After selling my business, we decided to move to Ireland, where we now live in the beautiful Irish Midlands with our daughter, two sons, and all our animals.

The grass really is greener over here (yep, it rains a lot!), and it's rich in culture and heritage. There's something to appeal to everyone, from historical monuments, Celtic landmarks, fabulous landscapes, beautiful rivers, and the ever-present Irish charm.

I wish I had an interesting story about how I got into cakes, but it's a common story. I was making cakes for my children's birthdays, and other parents started asking me to make cakes for their children, and it kind of grew from there. I fell in love with cake making, but it was hard to juggle a full-time job, family, and cakes. I dreamt of being able to do cakes all the time, but I was reluctant to give up a full-time job. Well, thanks to the economy, I got the chance to give it a try when my office was closed, and while I was terrified at the prospect of being unemployed, I was excited at the chance of doing more cakes. And more cakes there were!

I'm lucky enough to be doing cakes full time, as well as teaching around Ireland, overseas, and in my own studio, Novel-T School of Cake. There's a wonderful cake world out there; I've made incredible cake friends, and I've met so many of my cake heroes through competing in cake competitions, both nationally and abroad. There are endless possibilities in this wonderful, crazy cake world I found myself a part of. I'm looking forward to meeting you here in Sugarland too!

simply
EAR-ESISTABLE
by Tanya Ross

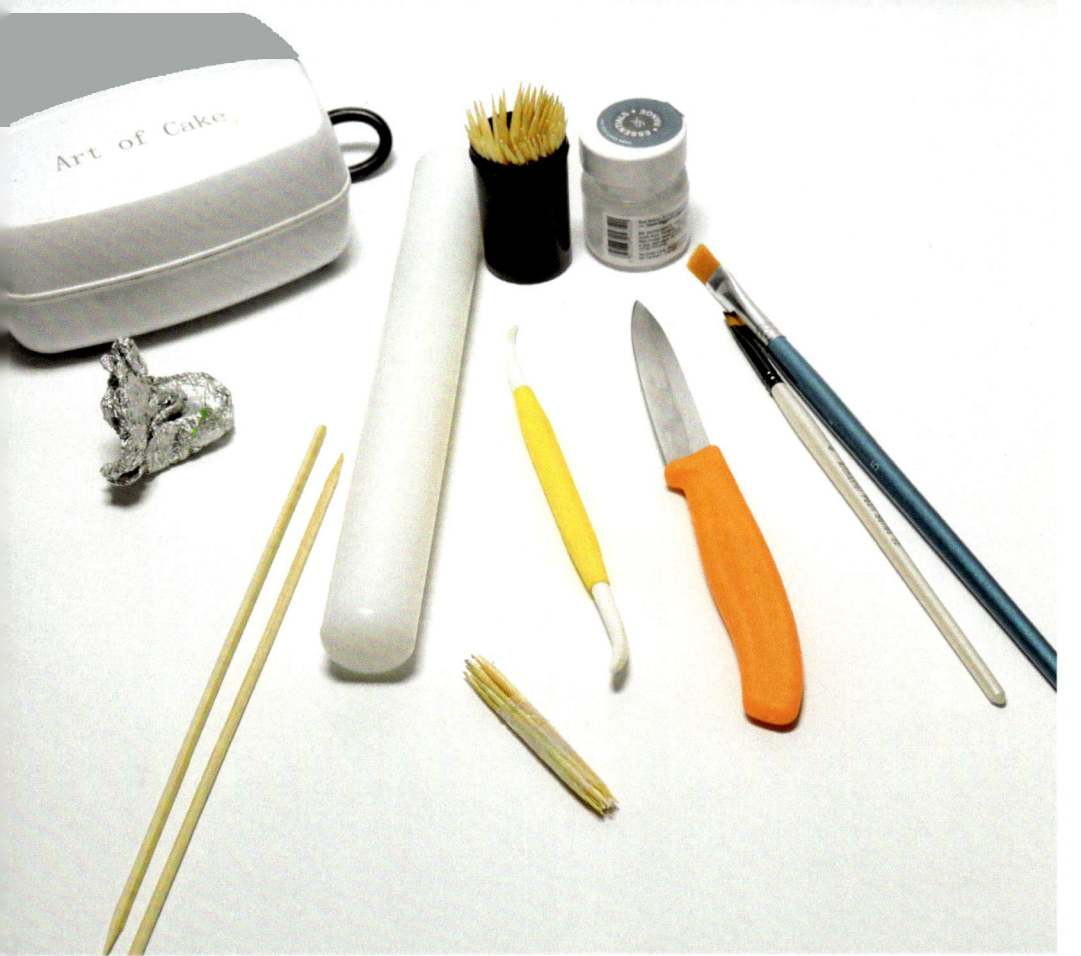

EQUIPMENT AND SUPPLIES

1X	10" square cake *(I used a 10" but use whatever size suits)*
1x	15" square cake drum
400g/14oz	Buttercream
1kg/35oz	Sugarpaste *(ivory makes a good base)*
10g/.5oz	Black sugarpaste for eyes
1x	Rolling pin
1x	Knife *(sharp with a thin blade)*
1x	Leaf veiner shaper tool *(Dresden tool)*
15x	Cocktail sticks
3x	Barbecue skewers
1x	4cm small polystyrene ball (or rice cereal treats shaped into a ball)
Edible glaze	*(Confectioner's glaze)*
Airbrush	You can dust the colours if you don't have an airbrush
Airbrush colours	Ivory and brown
Dusts	Dusky pink / Chocolate brown
Brushes	Flat paintbrush *(for dusting)* / Small paintbrush *(for glaze)*
Tin Foil	Aluminium Foil

1 Cut a square cake in half and join the halves with buttercream on the upright to make a higher rectangle.

2 To slope the body, cut off a triangle from the 2 top edges. Join the bigger (front) triangle at the base to extend the 'belly'.

3 Shape the belly by carving an indent at the hind leg and front leg to form a curve, tapering down towards the legs.

4 To make it look like the shape continues under the body, carve a little away on the back edge.

5 Crumb coat the entire shape in a thin layer of buttercream. Cover in sugarpaste slightly thicker than usual to allow texturing without tearing through.

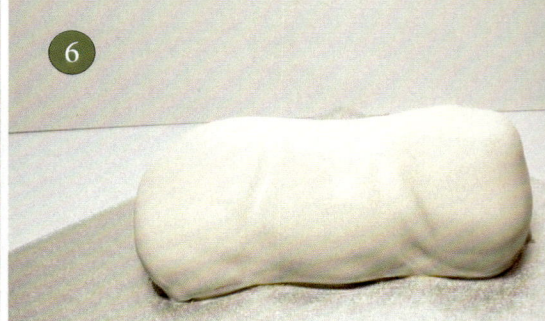

6 Using the back of the spoon-shaped Dresden tool, tuck in the bottom edges of the paste and accentuate the legs and butt.

7 Tightly tape a little bundle of cocktail sticks together to make a texturing tool. To create the fur texture, gently push the tool into the paste and twist it while pulling it out. Do this step while the paste is still fresh and not skinned over.

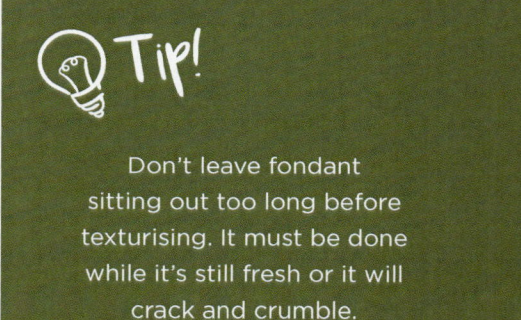

Tip! Don't leave fondant sitting out too long before texturising. It must be done while it's still fresh or it will crack and crumble.

8 To create longer hairs at the belly and back of legs, use the back of the pointy end of the Dresden tool.

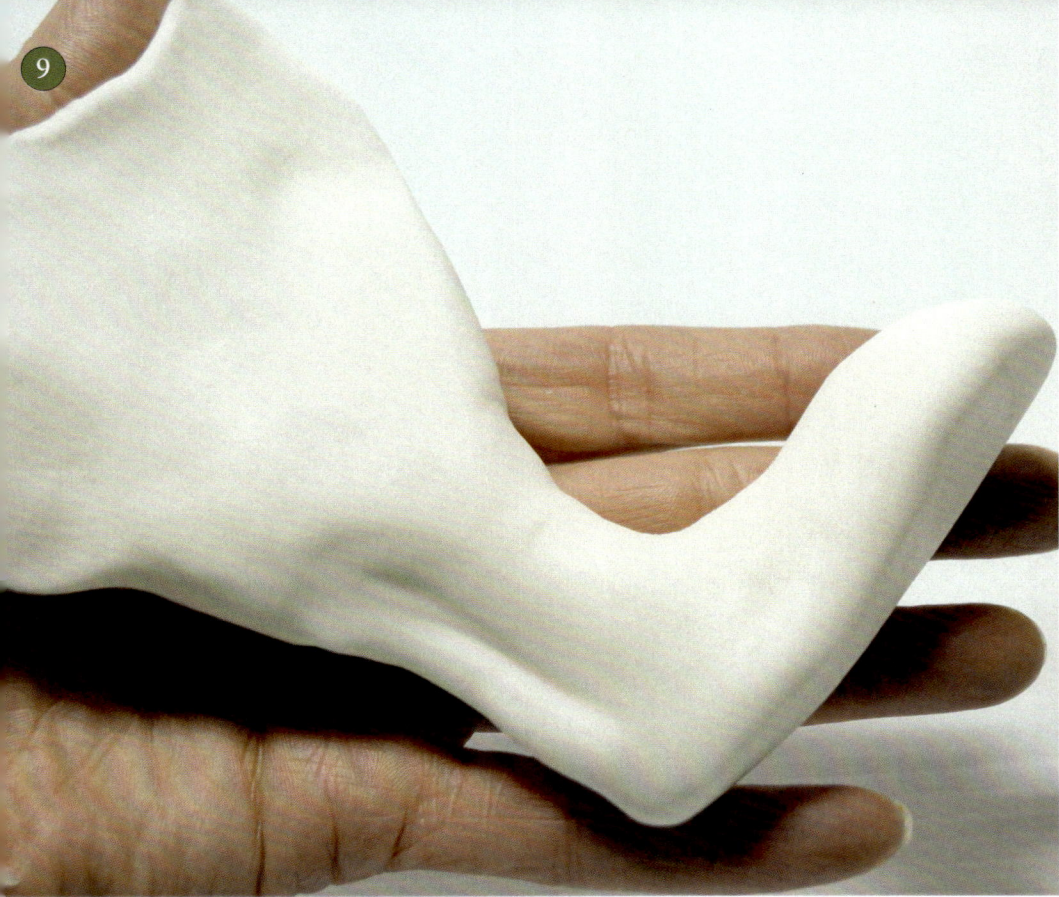

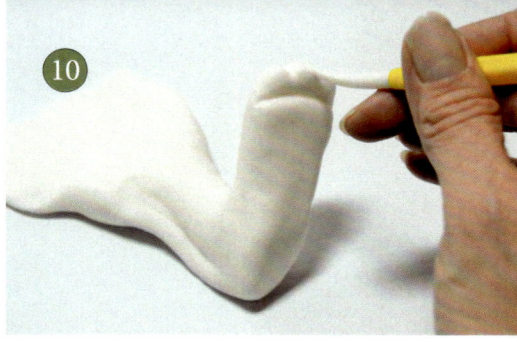

Using the Dresden tool, mark 3 toes and line underneath. Rub the edges to round the toes. Indent the heel to the back of the leg to show the tendon and gently squeeze in the arch of the foot with your thumb.

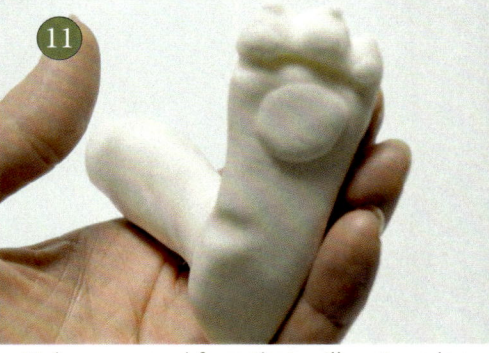

Make a second foot that will rest under the top hind leg.

Shape the hind legs a bit like drumsticks. Flatten the thigh so that it fits onto the haunch of the cake and shape the foot.

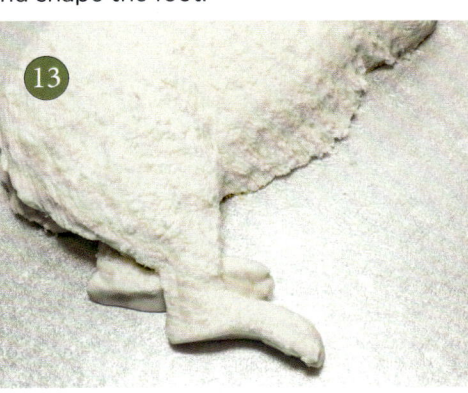

Attach the bottom leg to the cake and put the top leg in place. Using the spoon end of the Dresden tool, blend the join.

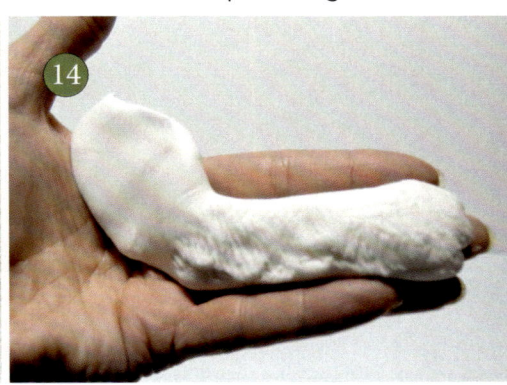

Texture the legs as before down to the top of the feet.

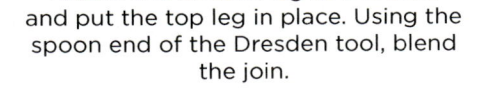

Roll sausages of sugarpaste for the front legs, shape the paws, and mark the toes with the back of the Dresden tool.

15 Attach the front legs to the body, blend in the joins, and texture using the same method as before.

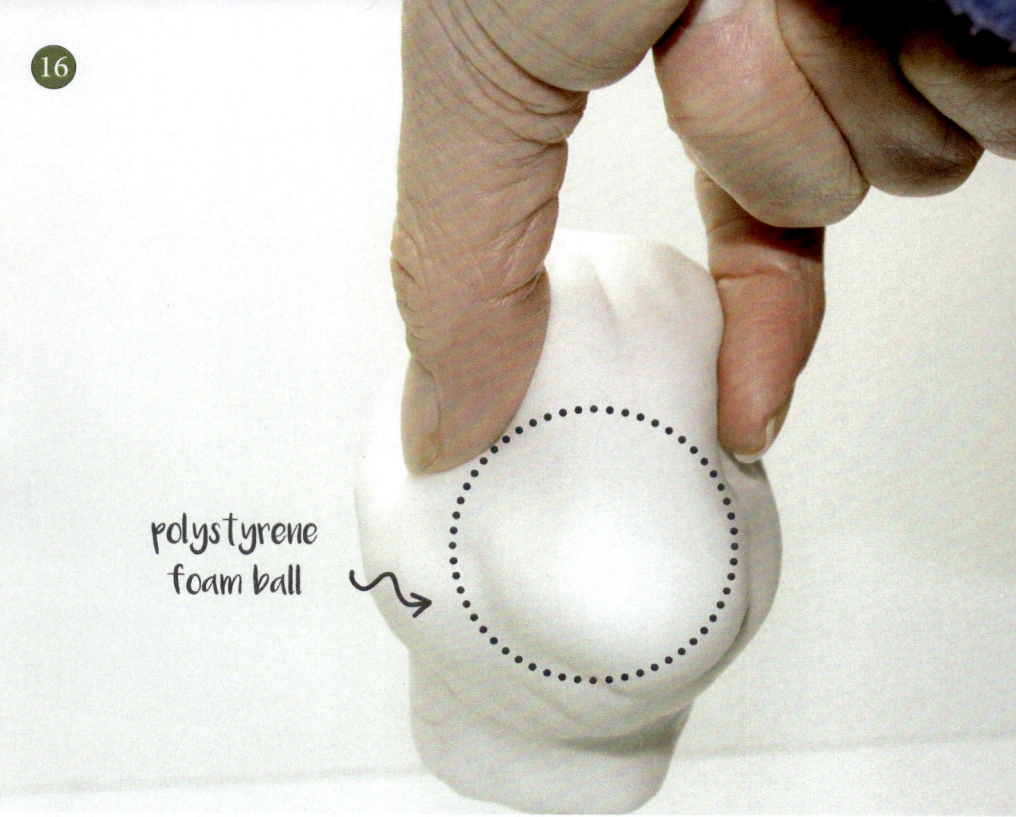

16 polystyrene foam ball

Shape the head over a polystyrene foam ball (or rice cereal treats) on a skewer for ease of handling.

17 Start with an egg shape and, with your thumb and forefinger, squeeze the top of sides to shape the eye sockets.

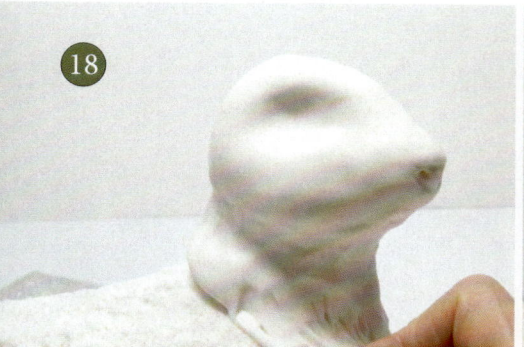

18 Cut a skewer to the height of the bunny's neck, place the head onto the body, and glue in place with water or edible glue. Roll out a sausage of paste to fill the gap.

19 Shape the neck and blend the joins between the torso and neck. Texture the neck and head as before.

20 Take 2 small balls of black paste, shape them into equal egg shapes, and place them in the eye sockets.

 **21**

Do not flatten the eyes, as you want them to have a curve.

 **22**

To shape the lower and upper eyelids, roll small sausages of paste for each eye.

 **23**

Use the Dresden tool to mark the eyelids (like eyeliner). Blend the joins and texture.

 **24**

Make a teardrop shape of sugarpaste for the tail. Attach the pointed end to the base of the spine and texture. Use the back of the Dresden tool to create longer hairs on the bottom of the tail.

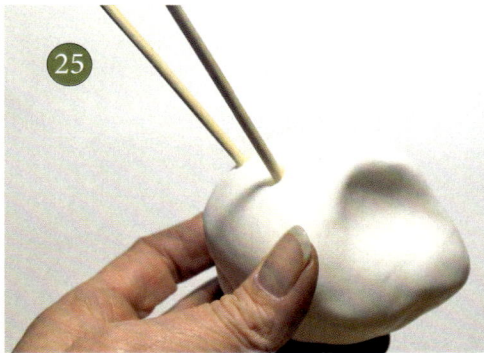 **25**

Measure skewers to support the ears. Insert them into the back of the head and into the foam ball or rice cereal treats for strength

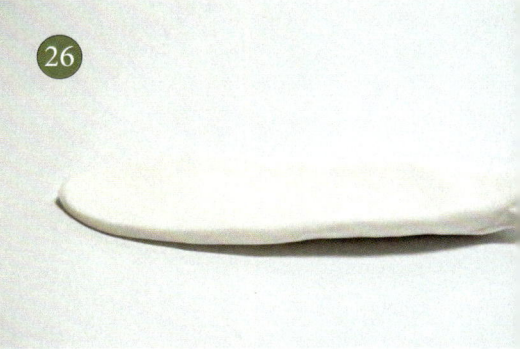 **26**

Using flower paste, shape the ears. Keep the base thick and get thinner towards the tips of the ears.

Push the ear onto the skewer and blend the joins. To keep the ears secure and to make them look real, curve the base of the ears in and blend towards the head.

Gently curve the top edge of the ear a little to give it a little movement. (You don't want a precise shape; bend it a little for a natural look).

If needed, add a small sausage of paste around the base and texture it so that the ear looks like it's coming out of the head rather than just stuck on.

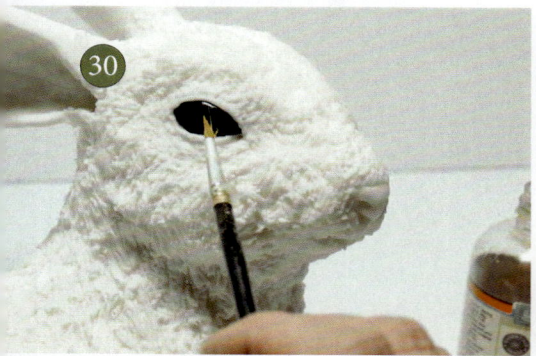

Paint a little edible glaze onto the eyeballs before airbrushing or dusting.

Airbrush a light undercoat of ivory over the whole rabbit, keeping it very light inside of the ears.

Spray brown lightly, leaving some ivory showing at the base of the belly, under the tail, and the back of the hind legs on the longer hair.

Once the airbrushing dries, use a flat brush and dust with chocolate brown dust, darken the creases of the legs, and shade the belly.

Dust some dusky pink on the inside of the ears and on the nose. The dust also highlights the fur texture and brings the bunny to life.

Give the eyes another coat of glaze and glaze the nose.

PRODUCTS USED IN THIS TUTORIAL
• Ice Wise Fondant
• Magic Colours™ Castle Grey

Cover your board with fondant. I used green and then used a scrunched-up piece of tinfoil to give a grassy texture. Sit back and look at your beautiful bunny cake!

Maria McDonald

Sugar Duckie Cake Design — Raheny, Dublin

Originally from Swords, Co. Dublin, the love of a good man encouraged me to pack my bags and migrate a whole 14 kilometres to Raheny, Dublin 5. There, we enjoyed many a coastal walk along the Bull Wall and Saturday afternoon food markets in glorious St Anne's park. A 15-minute DART ride to the City Centre meant that weekend brunches and catch-ups with friends in Dublin's fine eateries and pubs were a regular part of our lives. This idyllic, laid-back lifestyle was abruptly and rudely interrupted by the arrival of our beautiful triplet daughters, Olivia, Elise, and Jamie, in 2012.

The first two years of their gorgeous little lives were an excellent exercise in multi-tasking, sleep deprivation, and pushing limits. Armed with this training and new skills, the only natural progression was to take up cake decorating.

I made the girls a rather rough-around-the-edges fairy toadstool cake for their second birthday and never looked back. Still a hobbyist, I cake for fun under the name 'Sugar Duckie Cake Design'. Through caking, I discovered a love of sculpting, and I particularly enjoy modelling the human form. I also like to include a little humour in my work whenever I can—it's not unknown for me to chuckle my way through a project. Luckily for me, I'm easily amused.

ORANGE
You Happy?
by Maria McDonald

EQUIPMENT AND SUPPLIES

	6" ball tin
	10" drum covered in black
300g/10.5oz	Buttercream
400g/14oz	Dark chocolate ganache
	with a touch of Sicilian orange extract
200g/7oz	Fondant *(Select Ireland)*
100g/3.5oz	Vera Miklas™ modelling chocolate
10g/.35oz	Modelling paste
	Sharp knife
	Pallet knife
	Vinyl gloves
	Dresden tool
	Hair detangler hairbrush
	Nail brush
	Tin foil *(aluminium foil)*
	scrunched up into a ball
	Rolling pin
	Selection of fluffy brushes
	for dusting
	Selection of paintbrushes
	Airbrush
	Sugarflair yellow airbrush colour
	mixed with a touch of red

DUSTS
TO MIX WITH VODKA FOR PAINT

Black
White
Ice blue
Petal blue

TO DRY DUST WITH

Tangerine
Nut brown
Black
Burgundy
Flesh
Petal blue

Torte a 6" ball cake and fill with buttercream.

With your knife, draw a line around the top of the cake to use as a carving guide. An irregular line for the peel being removed from the orange looks more realistic.

Carve the cake above this line into a gentle point at the top. For a quicker cleanup, carve the cake on a sheet of cling film (plastic wrap).

Using the tip of your knife, carve out the facial features: 2 eyes and a mouth.

Slather the cake in some chocolatey ganache goodness, following the shape of the carvings.

 Tip!

The easiest way to smooth ganache on an irregular shape is to use a combination of a warm palette knife and gloved hands. Poke your fingers into those eyes and mouth to get definition. (If you listen closely, you'll hear him scream.)

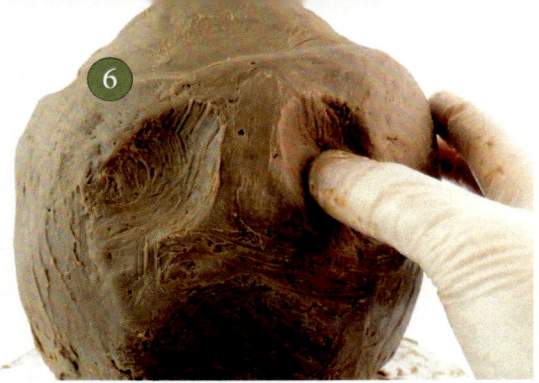

6 Coat the cake with ganache and pop it in the fridge for 10 minutes to set.

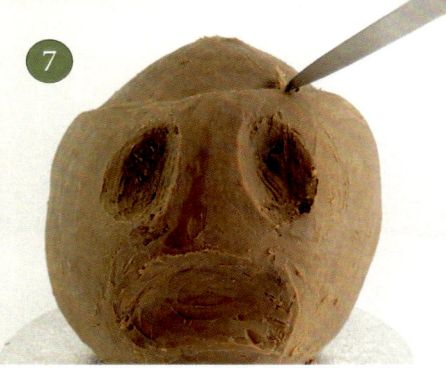

7 Use your knife to tidy up and define the edge where the peel will be. Keep the line irregular—there's no room for perfection on this project!

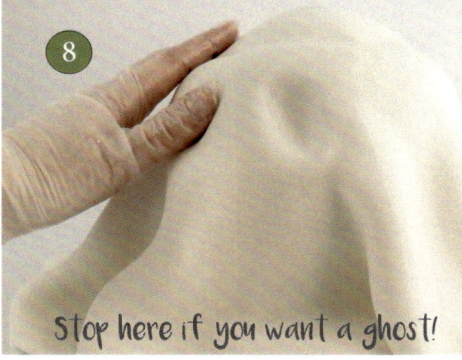

Stop here if you want a ghost!

8 Coat the cake in a thin layer of shortening. Roll out sugarpaste and cover the cake with it. Use gloved hands to smooth the paste into the features.

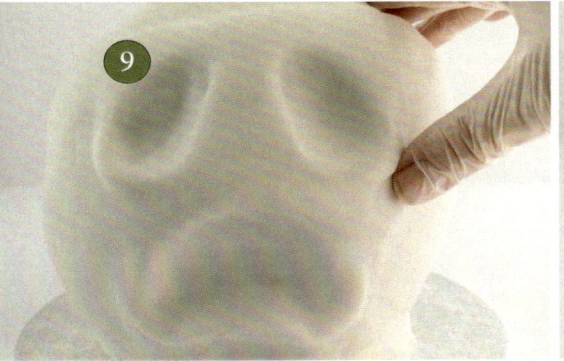

9 Gently press into the paste to create bags under the eyes and lips around the mouth.

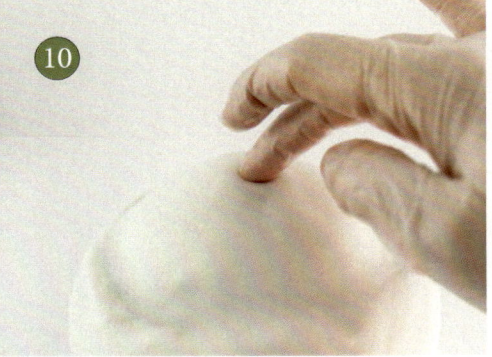

10 Dip your finger in the centre of the top where the orange segments separate.

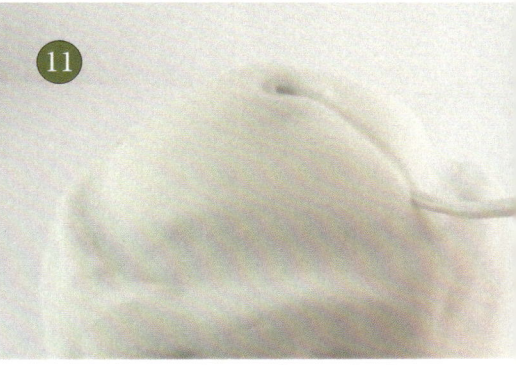

11 Using a Dresden tool, gently draw a line from the dip down to where the peel starts. Repeat the whole way around.

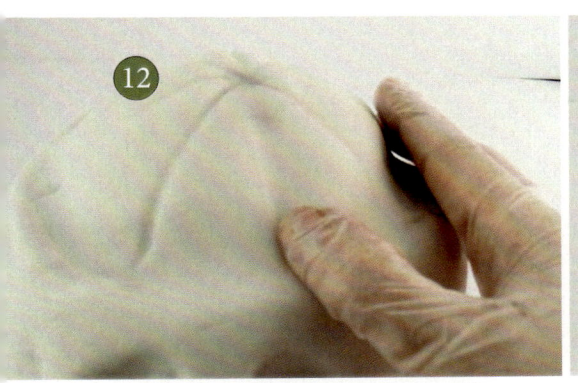

12 Gently soften these lines with your thumb.

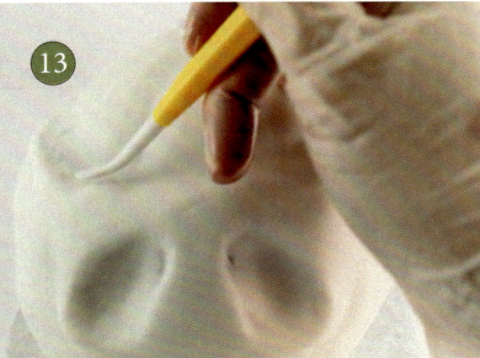

13 Add texture to the pith by roughing it up with the flat side of the Dresden tool.

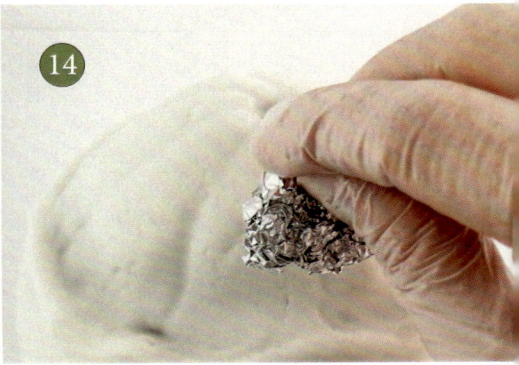

14 Loosely scrunch up a small ball of tinfoil and gently dab on the orange segments to give the impression of pith on the flesh.

15

Gently press a detangler into the orange skin. Adjust your pressure so that some dents are deeper than others.

16

And now we're ready for some colour!

17

Using an airbrush, spray the skin orange. Some overspray on the top will add to the look and save you colouring it later!

18

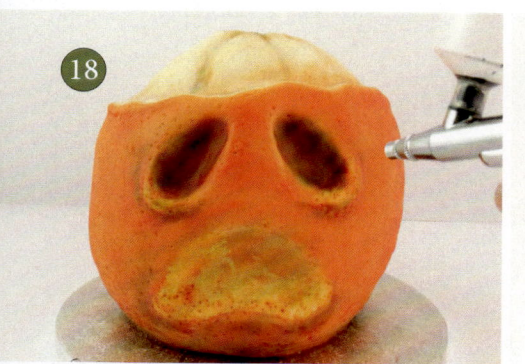

Spray the insides of the eyes black. (It should start to look a bit spooky.)

19

Using the sharp knife, cut the sugarpaste out of the mouth.

20

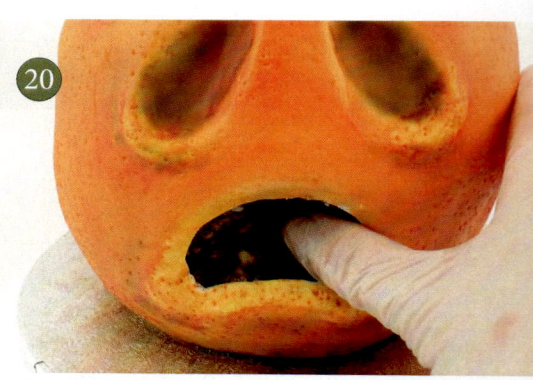

Gently push the cake back from the mouth. (Do this step before you put the teeth in so that you don't get bitten.)

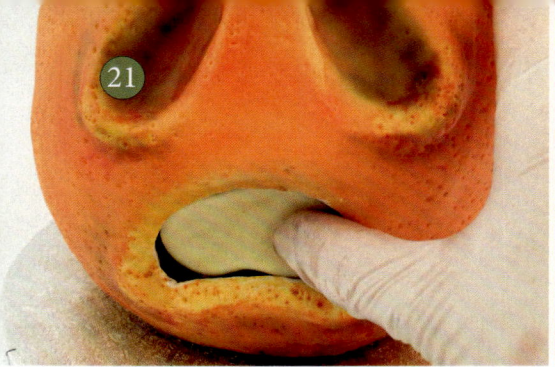

Press some modelling chocolate into the cavity and under the sugarpaste at the lips to seal the gap.

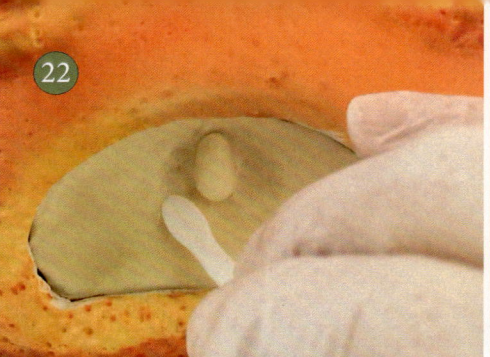

Make the epiglottis by adding a teardrop of modelling chocolate at the top centre of the cavity.

Draw an 'm' shape for the tongue. Push in the modelling chocolate above the tongue to give depth. Poke little holes into the tongue for texture.

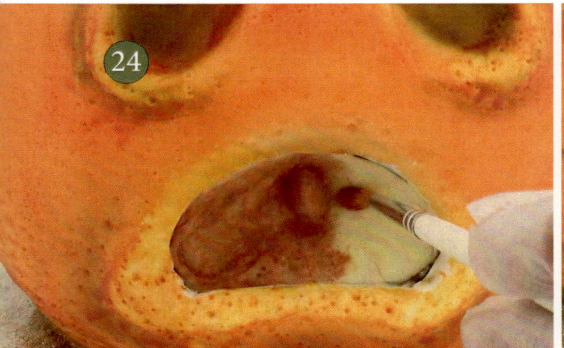

Mix the flesh-coloured powder with a drop of vodka or dipping solution to make a paint and colour the inside of the mouth.

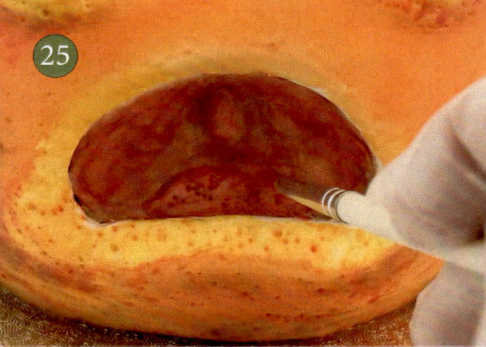

With a paintbrush, dab over the tongue and tonsil area with burgundy dust mixed with vodka. A few dabs will give a nice texture and depth of colour.

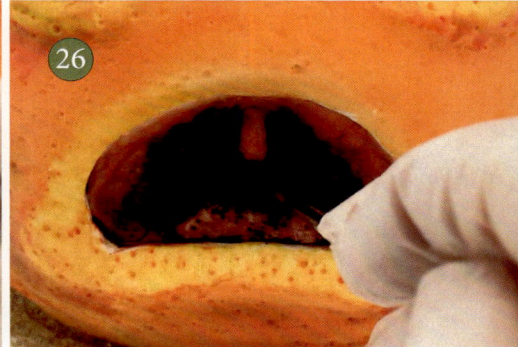

Paint the very centre of the mouth black. When dry, use a dry brush with a bit of black dust to shade the tongue and the centre of the mouth.

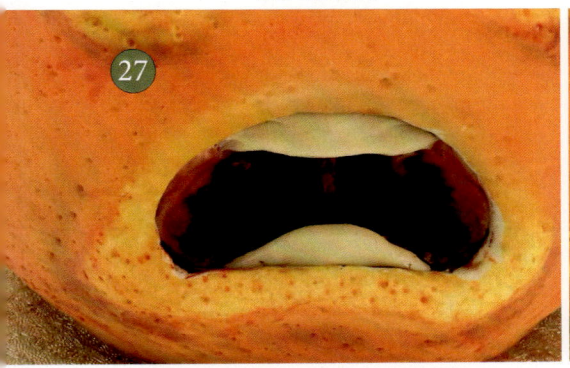

Cut a flattened strip of modelling chocolate into a rectangle and another into a crescent shape. Stick them to the inside of the lips, curving the edges towards the back of the throat.

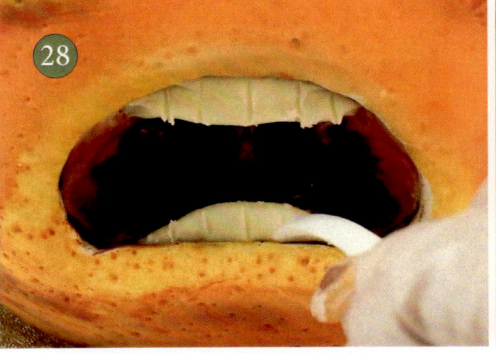

Using the Dresden tool, draw vertical lines on the teeth to outline his gnashers.

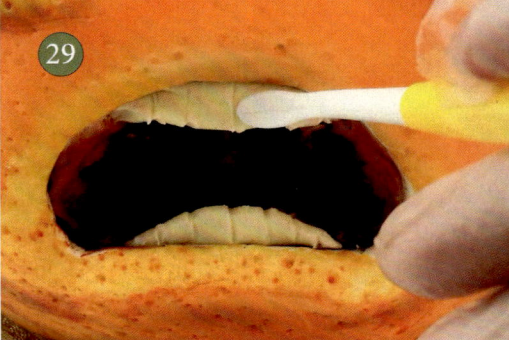

Gently shape the teeth with your Dresden tool. Press the back of the tool between each tooth to round off the edges and break up the straight line. No need for a full floss!

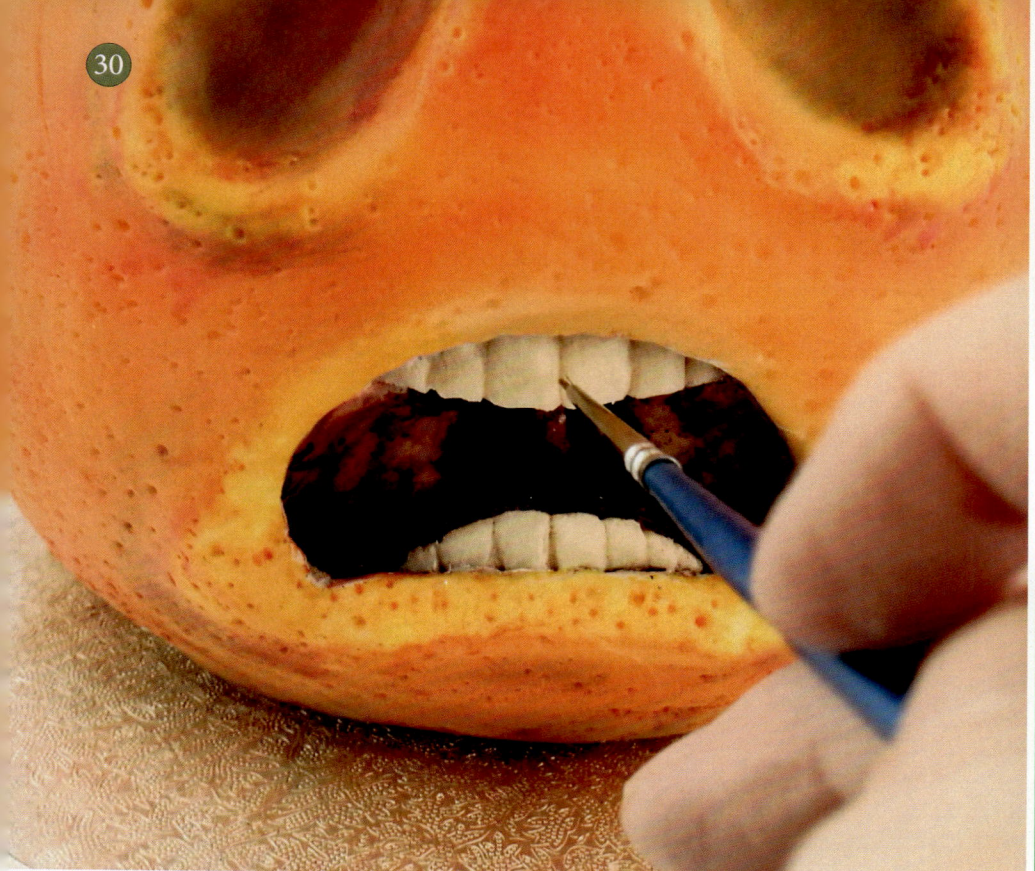

Roll a piece of white modelling paste into a ball.

Gently squeeze one end of the ball and flatten out this piece.

Whiten the teeth with a little white dust mixed with vodka. Then, using a fine brush dipped in a little brown dust, define the line between each tooth.

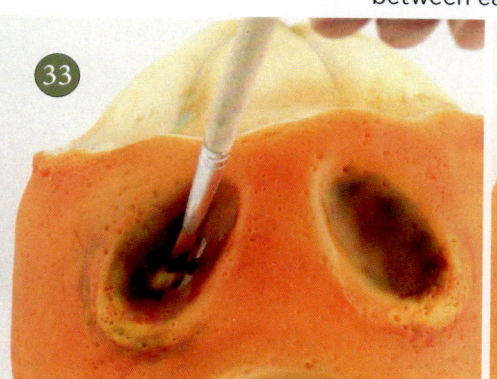

Dampen the eye sockets with some water.

Pop in the eyeballs and use the Dresden tool to shape them. Put a nice inward curve on the outside top of each eye to give our poor little fella a worried look.

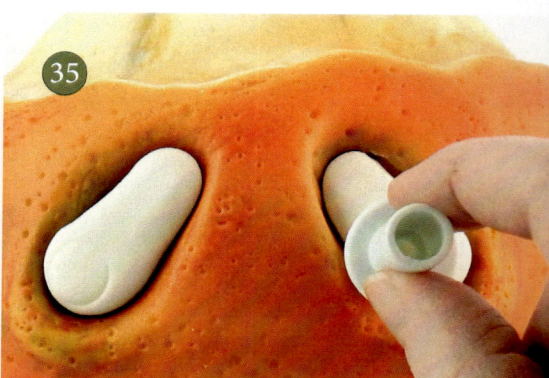

Outline the iris with a circle tool. This step isn't necessary if you have a careful hand, but my eyes always end up different sizes if I don't do this.

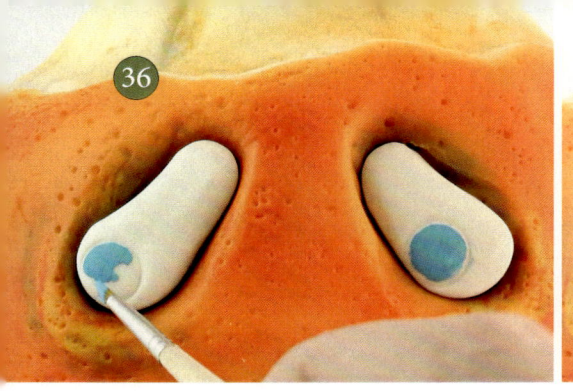

Paint the irises a pale blue.

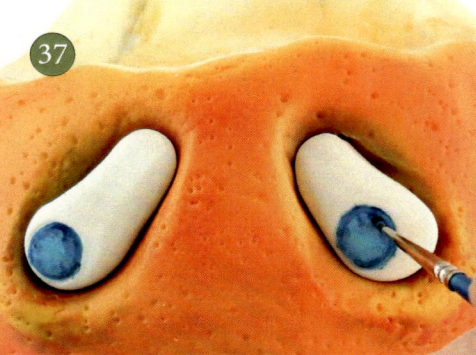

Outline the irises with a darker blue. Using little flicks, drag the paint towards, but not right into, the centre.

Outline the irises in black, paint in the pupils, and add little flecks of white. Now he can see!

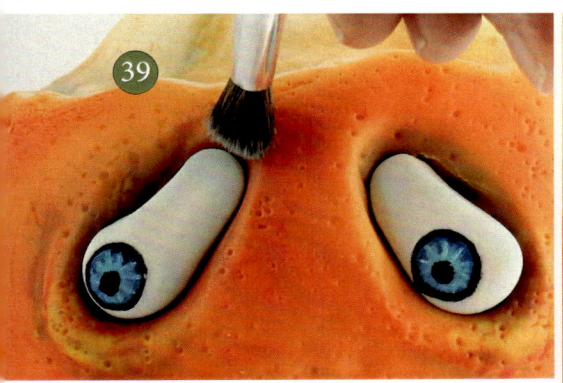

Using a fluffy dry brush, dust around the edges of the eyes with light blue dust to add depth.

Add 2 little teardrop shapes of white paste to the irises to add a sparkle. With a big, fluffy dry brush, dust around the bottom of the cake in brown.

Using a smaller dry brush, outline the sockets with black.

DRY DUSTING INSTRUCTIONS

Spill a little dust onto some kitchen towel. Load up your fluffy dry brush with the colour.

Tap off the excess onto a clean piece of the kitchen towel.

Dab onto your chosen area. You can build up the colour with more layers if needed.

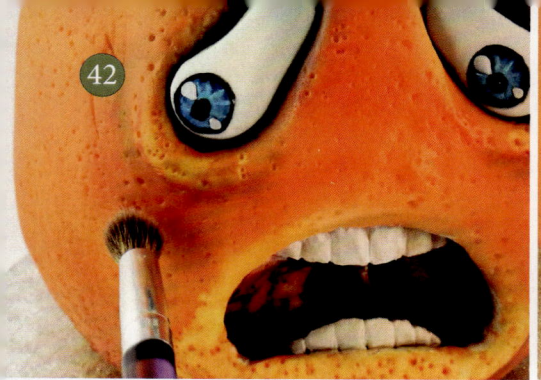

42 Shade under the eyes and lips with more brown dust to pick out the details.

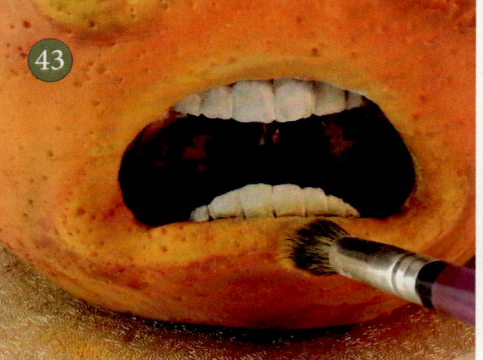

43 If you want, you can darken his lips with a deep orange dust.

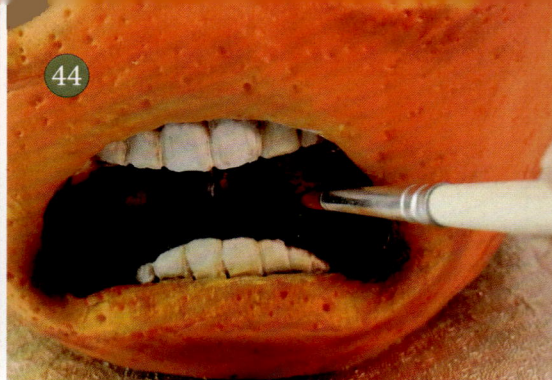

44 Have a look at where you might need to tidy up. Highlight the inside of the mouth with white paint or add shading to crevices if needed.

45 Paint little splotches onto the segments using the orange airbrush paint.

46 Dab the splotches off with some kitchen roll (paper towel).

47 Now onto the peel! Roll a piece of modelling chocolate into a sausage shape.

Maria McDonald — www.facebook.com/sugarduckie

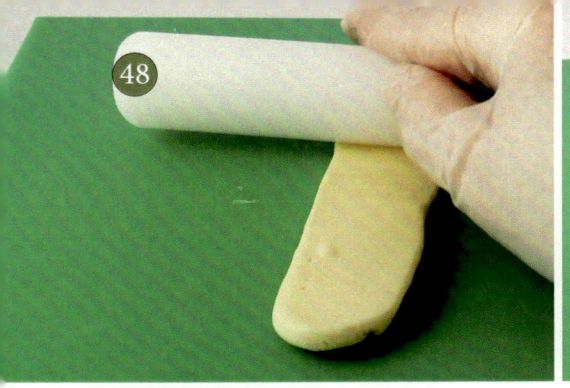

Flatten out the sausage to about 4mm with a rolling pin—not too thin.

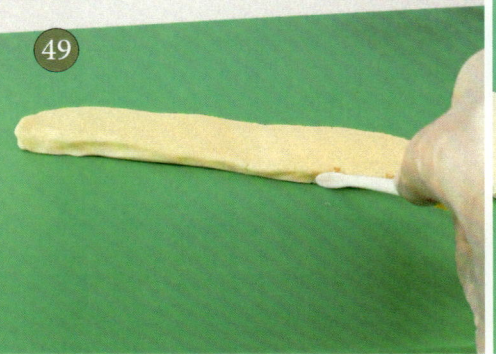

Using your Dresden tool, indent the sides to give it that ripped look.

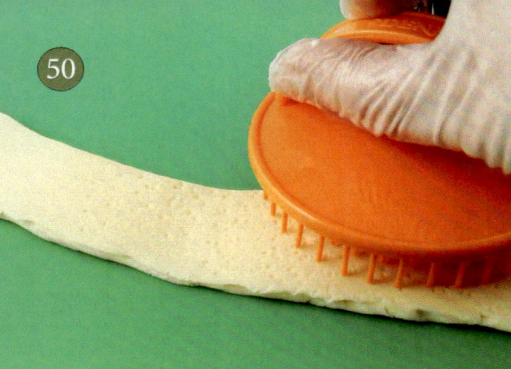

Using the same technique as earlier, texture one side with the detangler hairbrush.

Airbrush the skin orange.

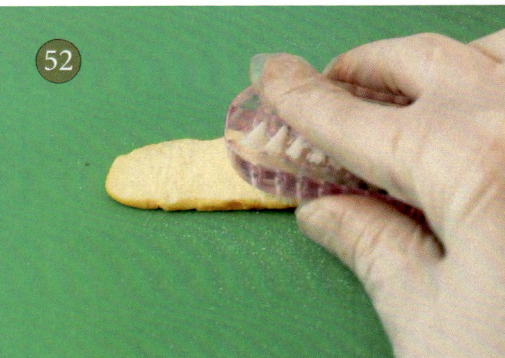

When dry, flip it over and bash it with a nail brush (only used for cake). Don't be afraid to rough it up a bit.

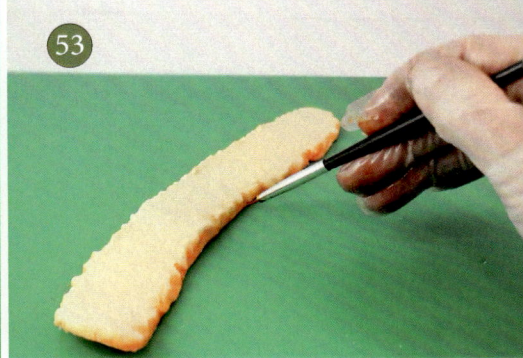

Dab a little orange airbrush colour along the edges of the skin.

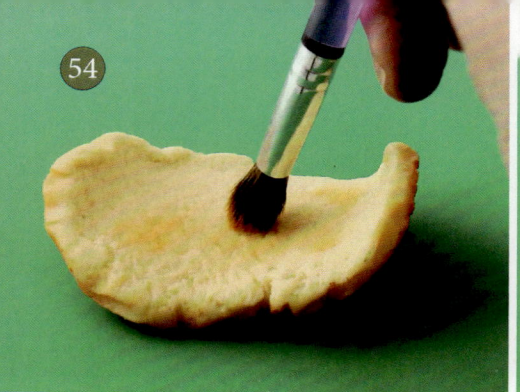

54

Dust a few splotches of orange onto the pith side of the skin (not too much though).

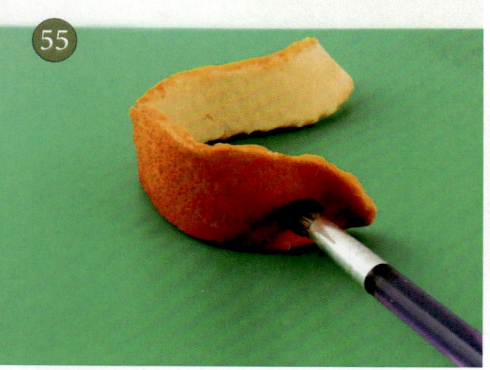

55

Curve the skin into an attractive shape and get into the crevices of the curve with some brown dust.

56

Place your cake and skins onto a covered board and have a chuckle!

Maria with her triplets Olivia, Elise & Jamie

Wooly Lamb

by Corinna Maguire

EQUIPMENT AND SUPPLIES

1x	12" wooden board
1x	4" cake drum
4x	4" bolts
12x	8mm nuts
12x	Wide 8mm washers
	Drill with 8mm screw-bit
4x	Nail-in furniture feet
	6" round ball cake
	(ball cake tin)
	Dark chocolate ganache
1700g/60oz	White fondant
	(Select Ireland)
340g/12oz	White modelling chocolate
	(Vera Miklas™) mixed with
	Castle Grey colour gel
315g/11oz	White modelling chocolate
	(Vera Miklas™) with green food colouring gel
90g/3oz	Dark modelling chocolate
	(Vera Miklas™) with
	Black food colouring gel
	Dish washing brush
	Dresden tool *(flower veiner)*
	Scissors
	Toothbrush *(or florist wires)*
	Plastic cake dowel
	Small flower press cutter
	Rolling pin
	Knit impression mat
	Confectioner's glaze

1 Prepare the cake board. Drill 4 holes in the shape of a 2.25" square into your cake board. Make sure the holes aren't too close to the edge.

2 Mark 4 corresponding dots using the holes from the cake board as a guide.

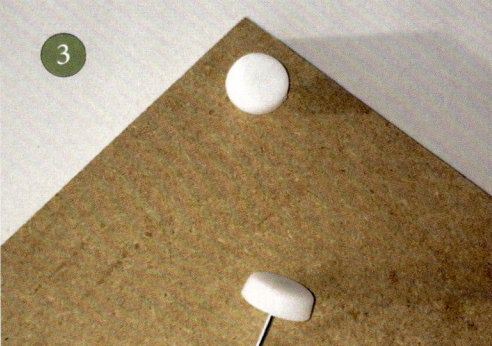

3 On the bottom side of the board, nail in four 'feet' to raise it up.

4 Insert each bolt from the underside, spaced with a washer.

5 On the top side, place another washer and nut. Tighten the 2 nuts together.

6 Add another 4 nuts to the top, with a washer above each. Keep the nuts level. These nuts will support the cake drum.

7 Mark one-half of the cake with the size of your cake drum.

8 Cut off the excess so that the cake will sit flush on the cake board.

9 Flip the cake upside down and spread the filling in between the 2 layers of cake.

10 Place the second half of the cake on top.

11 Fit the cake board onto the 4 screws and sit it level on the washers. Fill the exposed holes with fondant.

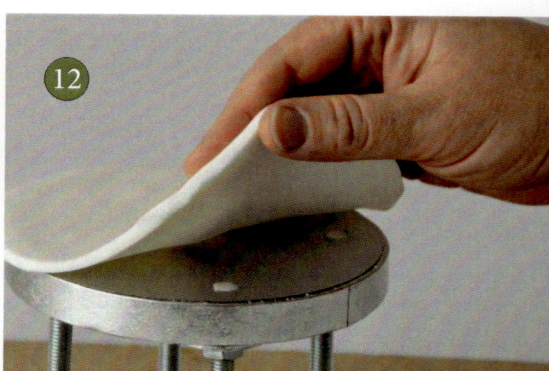

12 Place a layer of fondant on the cake drum. Secure the fondant into place with a bit of water.

13 Spread some ganache onto the layer to secure the cake on top.

14 Fill the gap between the layers with more ganache.

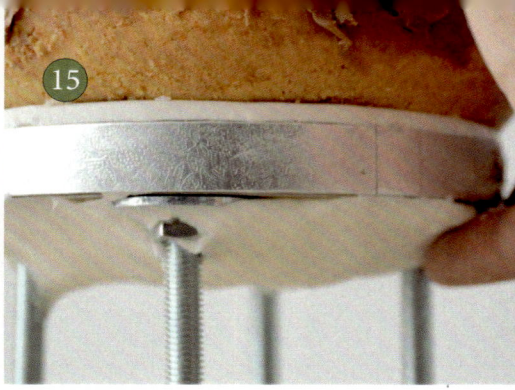

15 Using water or edible glue, securely place a dome of white fondant under the cake drum.

16 Using a flexi smoother, spread your ganache onto the cake. You can bend it slightly to follow the curve of the cake as you smooth it on. Don't forget to blend in cake down to the cake board so that there isn't a hard edge.

17 After the ganache has hardened, spray or paint some water onto it to give the fondant something to stick to.

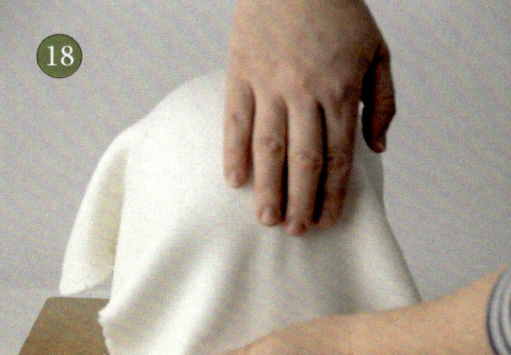

18 Roll out white fondant large enough to cover the whole sphere. Cover the cake and smooth out the top pleats.

19

Work your way down the cake, opening out and smoothing down the pleats.

20

Continue smoothing the fondant as low as you can.

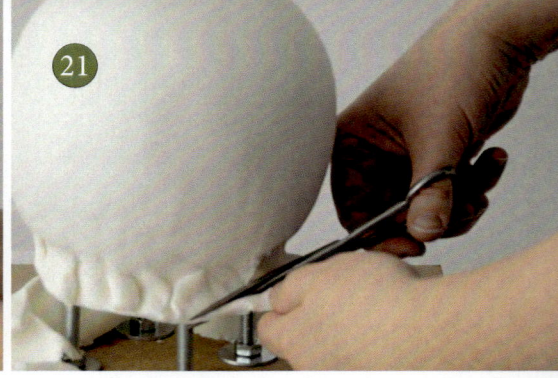

21

Remove any excess fondant that might be too heavy and might tear. Then continue to smooth out the pleats.

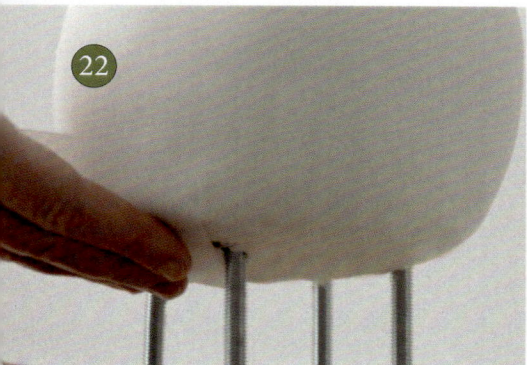

22

Join up and smooth the fondant to the panel attached to the underside of the cake board.

23

To make the lamb's legs, start by mixing some grey food colouring gel into the white modelling chocolate until you get a streak-free, medium-grey colour.

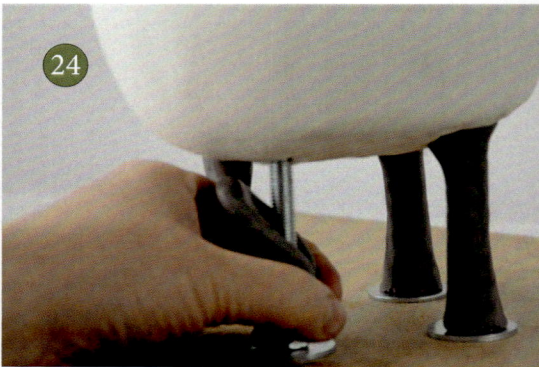

24

Roll sausages of the grey modelling chocolate. Cut a slit lengthways into the legs, and wrap the legs around the bolts.

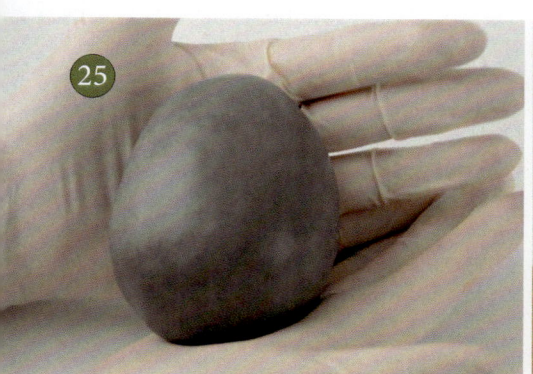

25

To make the lamb's head, roll out grey modelling chocolate (around 250g) into an egg shape.

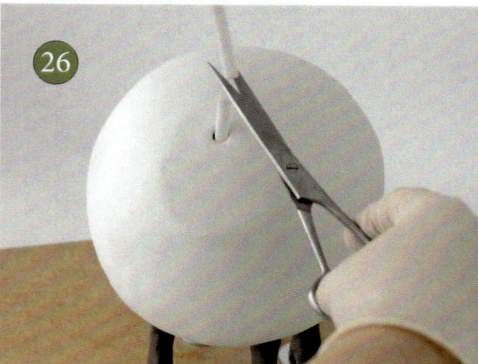

26

Once you know where you're placing the head, insert a food-safe plastic dowel into the cake to support the head's weight.

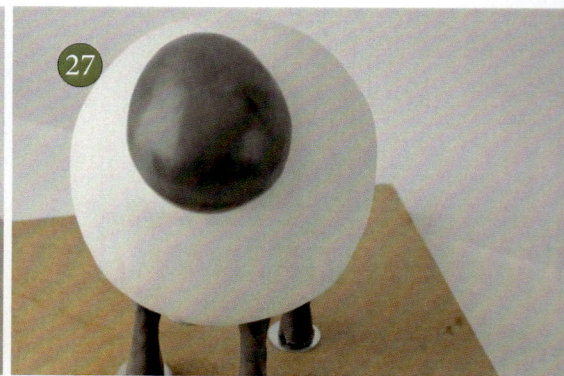

27

Place the head onto the dowel, and secure it into place with some water or edible glue.

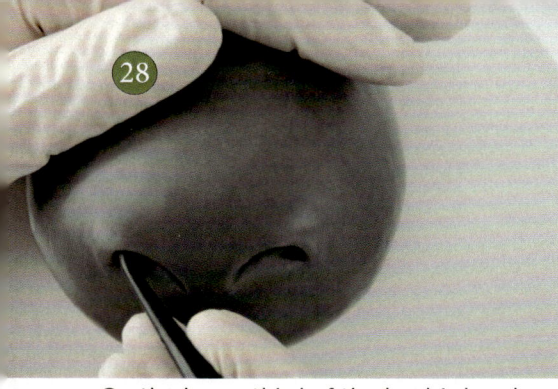

On the lower third of the lamb's head, make 2 slits and pull outwards gently on each to make the lamb's nostrils.

Now for the lamb's curls! Roll out tapered sausages of white fondant and coil them up onto themselves. A variety of sizes, coiling in different directions will add to the effect. This is the time-consuming part, but it gives a great texture.

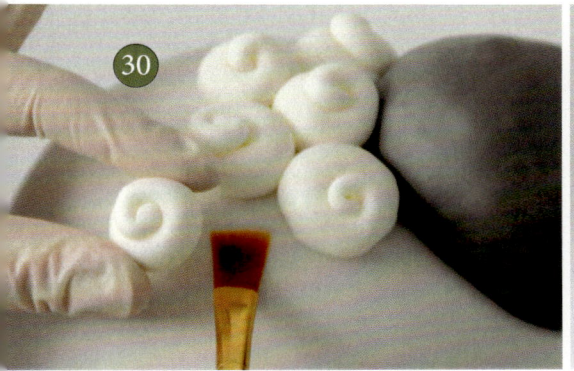

Make the curls in small batches to stop cracking. Secure each curl into place with a bit of water.

Continue until the entire body is covered in curls. You can leave the underside bare if you prefer (or can't be bothered)!

To make the lamb's scarf, colour some modelling chocolate green and use a knit-texture mat.

Roll out a piece of the green modelling chocolate, and place it on the mat. Roll over the chocolate to mark it with the texture.

Flip the mat over, and peel it off of the modelling chocolate.

Cut a couple of sections out of the chocolate for the scarf, with 1 section cut diagonally.

36

Wrap each of the triangle pieces around the neck, with the fat ends at the chin. Cut away any curls to fit it in place.

37

38

Take another smaller piece and place it underneath the other side of the scarf.

Place a rectangular section of scarf into the join at the lamb's chin, and tuck it in. Secure each of these sections into place with some water or edible glue. Try not to lose the pattern of the knit while working with these pieces.

39

For the fringe, roll out a piece of green modelling chocolate and measure the length that you need.

40

Cut a fringe into this section, making sure that the top part still holds them altogether.

41

Attach the fringe to the base of the scarf with a little water.

42 Repeat on the second scarf flap and cover the seams with another small strip of knit.

43 For the lamb's hat, using the template at the end of the tutorial as a guide, cut triangular sections away from a large panel of knit.

44 Use a little water to get the edges to stick together.

45 Make sure that the edges are secure. Try to be gentle so that you don't ruin the knit pattern.

46 Continue pinching the edges together until they fully join together in the centre.

47 For the pom-pom, add a ball of green modelling chocolate to the top.

48 For the lamb's eyes, using a medium ball tool, make 2 indentations in the lamb's head.

49 Insert 2 balls of black modelling chocolate that are just large enough to fill the indentations.

50 For the lamb's ears, roll 2 teardrops of the grey modelling chocolate and flatten them down.

51

Secure the top of each ear to the top of the lamb's head. I like to point them slightly forwards.

52

Place the lamb's hat onto its head and make a mark where it will sit.

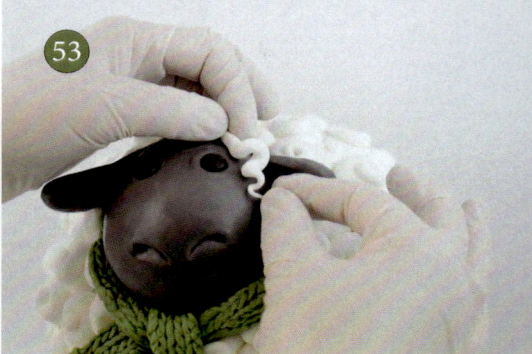

53

Curl some more pieces of white fondant and place them just inside the marked line of where the hat will be.

54

Once you're happy with the lamb's extra curls, place the hat on top of the curls, making sure that the hat is securely in place.

55

For the lamb's eyelids, cut out a circle the size of the eye socket. Cut this circle in half and place each half on the top half of each eye.

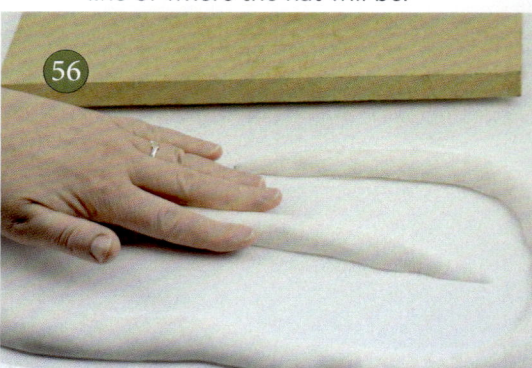

56

Roll a very long sausage of white for the board. Flatten down the base of the sausage so that there's a good surface area to attach the grass to.

57

Place in a coil around the lamb's legs. Paint water underneath to stick it to the board and all over the top to help the grass stick to the board.

58

Thickly roll green fondant and use a dish brush to pound into it until it looks like mossy grass. Place the grass in pieces around the white base, starting with the area between the lamb's legs.

59

It's a good idea to dust the area underneath with corn flour or icing sugar as it can stick to the surface during this process.

60 Add each piece of grass in sections until the whole board is covered.

61 Cut off the excess grass from the edges of the board.

62 Blend in the seams using a dish brush to texturise the seams together.

63 Use a firm toothbrush to blend in hard-to-reach areas.

64 You can also bend a stack of florist wires to blend in the hard-to-reach seams.

65 For the hooves, cut out 4 ribbons of the black modelling chocolate, and wrap them around the base of each leg.

66 Cut a slit into each of the hooves to give the lamb a 'cleft' foot.

67 OPTIONAL: You can paint the hat and scarf with another shade of green to give it more of a two-tone effect.

68 To decorate the board, using a small flower cutter or press and some white fondant, cut out a few little flowers.

69 Place a small circle of coloured modelling chocolate into the centre of each flower.

70 Place 1 more flower on the side of the lamb's 'mouth' as though it's chewing on it.

71 Finally, bring the lamb to life by glazing the eyes with some confectioner's glaze.

knit effect options

If you don't have the knit mat, you can still create a similar effect. These techniques might take a little longer to make, but you'll still be more than happy with the results.

Extruder Technique

Hand Technique

EXTRUDER TECHNIQUE
Use a good extruder and the three-leaf shamrock disc attachment. Extrude a length of modelling chocolate a little longer than the length that you need, and twist it clockwise. Repeat with a second length, and twist it clockwise.

HAND TECHNIQUE
Roll out two equally thick sausages of modelling chocolate and twist them together clockwise. Repeat with another two, twisted in the opposite direction.

TO FINISH
Attach the two lengths together, making sure that they are twisted in towards each other. Use a bit of water if needed. Continue making these pairs, and join them together until you have enough to create the scarf and hat for the lamb.

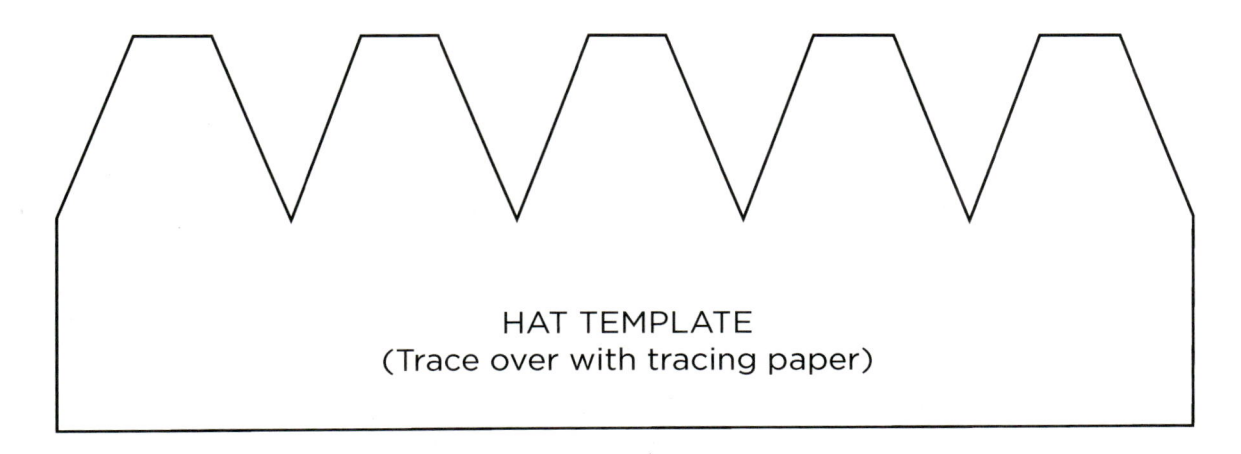

HAT TEMPLATE
(Trace over with tracing paper)

(Baaa!)

**PRODUCTS USED
IN THIS TUTORIAL**
- Vera Miklas™ Modelling Chocolate in both White and Dark
- Select Ireland White Fondant
- Magic Colours® Castle Grey
- ProGel® Black
- ProGel® Forest Green
- Knit Simpress Marvelous Mold™
- Makin's® Clay Extruder

"Mistakes are the portals of discovery."
James Joyce

ADVANCED
TUTORIALS

The Dark Hedges, County Antrim, Northern Ireland
Photograph by (Uncle) Graeme Longmuir

Emma Stewart

Truly Scrumptious Cakes by Design — Omagh, Co. Tyrone

I never really set out to be a caker, but I fell into it. I actually have a HND Biomedical Science and a BSc (Hons) Sports Therapy...so cakes are about as far away from my education as you can get. My inspiration has always been and always will be my Grandpa. He made cakes as a young man until he had to give it up. His passion and heart were still in cakes even when he couldn't make them.

I made my very first cake back in September 2010 for my eldest son's first birthday. Two years later, after a lot of practise, I made my friend's wedding cake. At the time, I had left my full-time job to be a child minder and fell pregnant with my youngest son. After I had my son, I never went back to child care as the cakes just took off.

I'm originally from Maidstone in Kent, England, but I was born in Chatham, where the maritime dockyards are.

I met my husband, Stephen, at university in Luton. Stephen is from a small town called Omagh in County Tyrone in Northern Ireland. When we finished university in 2005, we moved to Omagh, and we've been here since.

The way of life in Omagh is far more relaxed than in Maidstone, and everyone here knows nearly everyone else—or at least someone who knows them. There's so much stunning scenery and places to visit, though you have to accept that there's always a chance of showers with any sunshine that we have.

midnight Flame
by Emma Stewart

EQUIPMENT AND SUPPLIES

CAKE

	5" Round cake *(5" tall)*
	7" Round cake *(5" tall)*
	10" Round cake drum
	5" Round cake card
1kg/35oz	White fondant
	Large rolling pin
	Solid plastic smoother
	Sharpened wooden dowel
	Flexi smoother set
	Sharp knife
	Turntable
	Graphite lustre
	(Faye Cahill)
	High-percentage alcohol
	such as dipping solution
2x	Natural bristle brushes
	Extra large 'fluffy' brush
1tsp	Royal icing
4x	Plastic dowels
	Acupuncture needle

FLOWERS

100g/3.5oz	White sugar florist paste
100g/3.5oz	Green sugar florist paste
30g/1oz	Burgundy sugar florist paste
	Foam pad
	Medium-sized ball tool
	Dresden tool

Small rolling pin
Veining board
56mm 5-petal cutter
30mm rose petal cutter
*squeezed to elongate
to 44mm long*
46mm rose petal cutter
Cosmo petal veiners
25mm CelBud
*attached to a 1/3 length
of 20-gauge wire*
5x   26-gauge white wire
cut into 3
Medium calyx cutter
Rose leaf cutters
Dahlia petal cutters
Universal lead veiner
5x   28-gauge green wires
cut into 3
5x   26-gauge green wires
cut into 3
Edible glue
X-Acto® knife or blade
Green floral tape
White floral tape
Straw or posy pick
or safety seal
Selection of brushes
for dusting
Edible glaze

COLOURS

DAHLIA AND ALSTROEMERIA
Lemon Tart petal dust *(Rainbow Dust)*
Flame Red petal dust *(Rolkem)*
Cherry Pie petal dust *(Rainbow Dust)*
Spring Green petal dust *(Rainbow Dust)*
Chocolate Brown edible pen
(Magic Colours™)

LIGHT BERRIES
Pink Candy petal dust *(Rainbow Dust)*
Spring Green petal dust *(Rainbow Dust)*

DARK BERRIES
Claret petal dust *(Rainbow Dust)*
Aubergine petal dust
Blackcurrant petal dust *(Rolkem)*

LEAVES
Raw Amber petal dust *(Rolkem)*
Olive petal dust *(Rolkem)*
Foliage Green petal dust
Spring Green petal dust *(Rainbow Dust)*
Autumn Green petal dust *(Rainbow Dust)*
Claret petal dust *(Rainbow Dust)*

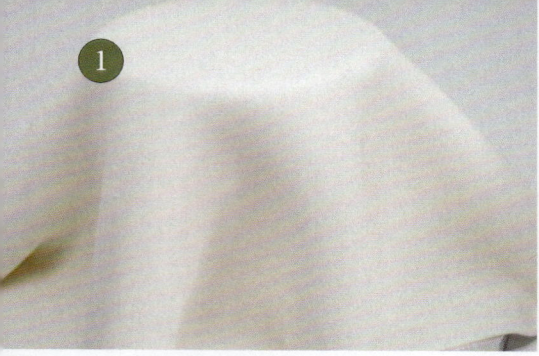

1 Level, fill, and coat each cake with either ganache or buttercream. Attach the 5" cake to the cake card with ganache. Roll fondant to approximately 4mm thick.

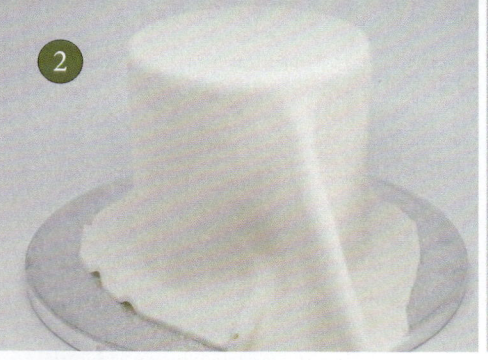

2 Lightly dampen the surface of the cake with water and lay the fondant over it. Smooth the top surface and then work around the sides of the cake.

3 Pull the fondant 'skirt' away at the base of the cake whilst smoothing to prevent folds or creases. Make a cut to 1 side of the fold.

 **Tip!**

For tiers where the height is equal to or greater than the width, use the 'back seam' method. Smooth the sides and gather the excess fondant into one fold. Make a cut to one side of the fold, lay the excess fondant across it, and straight cut to create a join. Blend the join using your hands and smoothers.

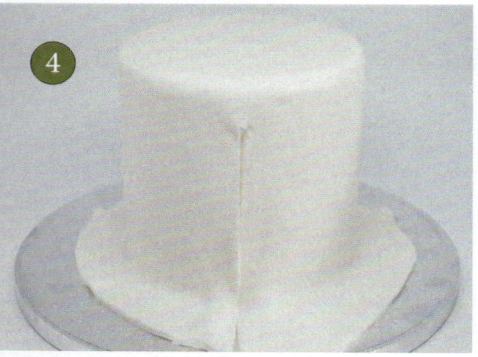

4 Lay the excess fondant across it and straight cut to create a join.

5 Blend the join using your hands and smoothers.

6 Use a solid plastic smoother to firmly attach the fondant to the sides of the cake and push it down to the base.

7 Use a sharpened wooden dowel to 'draw' around the base of the cake. This impression is a guide to create a clean cut with the sharp knife. Remove the excess fondant.

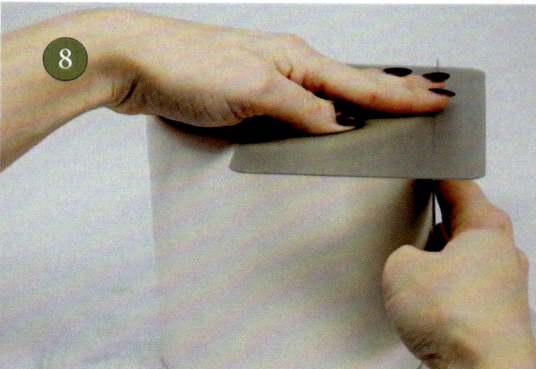

8 Using the flexi smoothers, gently rub the side of the cake until it's smooth. Remove any air bubbles by piercing them with an acupuncture needle.

9

Rest 1 smoother on top of the cake with 1/4" width overhanging. Lightly hold this overhang in place while smoothing the side.

10

Make sure that the smoothers are touching at a right angle at all times.

11

Too much pressure will cause a 'lip' or 'ring' to form at the top edge, so less is more.

12

Keep going until the edge appears sharp. To sharpen further, gently pinch your fingers and the smoothers towards each other.

13

Using the graphite lustre and high-percentage alcohol such as dipping solution, create an edible paint and place your cake on a turntable.

14

Using a wide, natural-bristled brush loaded with lustre solution, paint your way down the cake: start at the top of the and turn the turntable as you make your way down.

15

16

Repeat this process until the colour coverage is an even depth. Getting an even colour usually takes 3 coats.

17

Use a dry brush to go over the cake in the same motion. This technique evens out the colour and speeds up the drying process.

Once dry, lightly use a large, dry, fluffy brush with small, fast movements while turning the turntable to create a high shine all over the cake.

18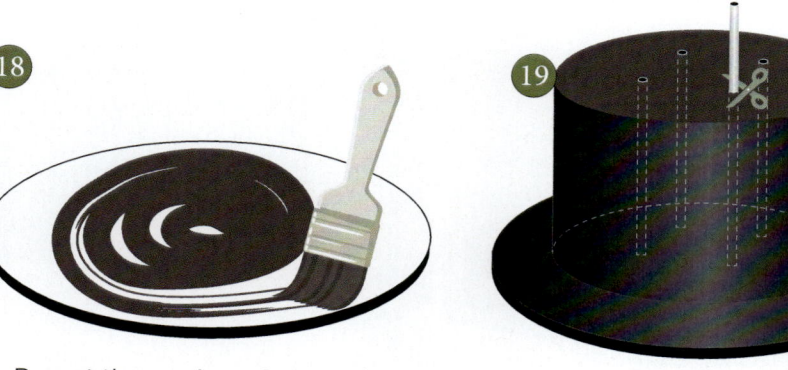

Repeat the previous steps on the second cake. Then cover the 10" cake board with white fondant and dry lustre it with graphite using the same method from the cakes.

19

Attach the 7" cake to the cake board using royal icing. Insert 4 evenly spaced dowels and cut them to height to support the 5" cake. Attach the 5" cake using royal icing.

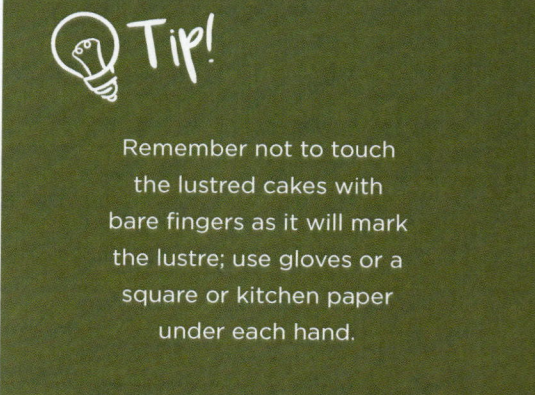

💡 Tip!

Remember not to touch the lustred cakes with bare fingers as it will mark the lustre; use gloves or a square or kitchen paper under each hand.

Dahlia

20 Roll a small ball of white sugar florist paste out to 1–2mm thick. Use a 56mm 5-petal cutter and lay out the cut onto a foam pad.

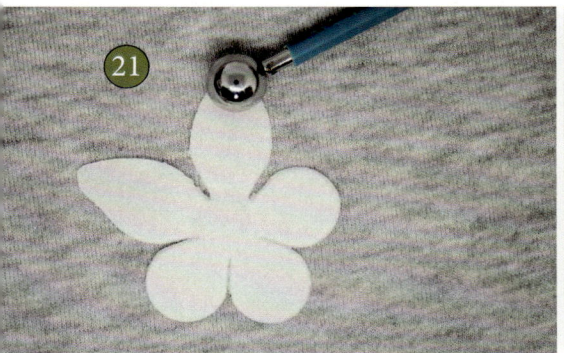

21 Using the ball tool, soften the petal edges by rolling the ball half over them on the petal. Then use the ball tool to stretch the petal to lengthen it.

22 Use the Dresden tool to add 2 vein lines to each petal. Add a small amount of edible glue at the base of each petal and fold in the lower edges.

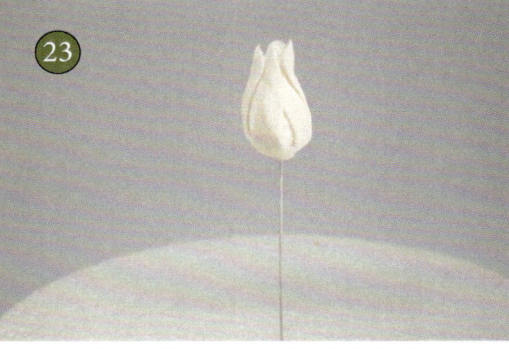

23 Attach the first layer of petals to the CelBud by feeding the wire through the petal's centre, then wrap the petals up around the CelBud and secure them with edible glue.

24 Repeat steps 20 and 21 twice but stretch the petals a little larger. Vein and fold as before. Add a little edible glue to the centre on 1 layer and attach the second layer above.

25 Add edible glue to the centre and lower the folded part of each petal. Then feed the petals onto the wire and apply gentle pressure to secure them to the first layer.

26 Repeat the previous 2 steps, increasing the petal size by stretching them further. Once attached, leave the to fully dry.

Once the dahlia is dry, use a medium-sized soft brush to dust it all over with Lemon Tart petal dust.

Add shading to the deep areas of the flower and between the petals using the Flame Red and Cherry Pie dusts.

Cut a medium-sized calyx and soften the edges with the ball tool on the foam pad. Thread the calyx onto the dahlia with edible glue and let dry before dusting with Spring Green and Foliage Green.

Steam the dahlia and let dry. Wrap the wire in green floral tape. Secure the tape at the calyx by pinching it round the wire. Wrap the tape around the wire's end.

Alstroemeria

Take 2 28-gauge white wires and cut each into 3. Roll 6 small balls of white sugar florist paste, glue 1 ball to the end of each wire, and taper them into an oval to form the stamen. Leave to dry. Tape the 6 stamens together using the white floral tape, starting approximately 1" below the head of each stamen.

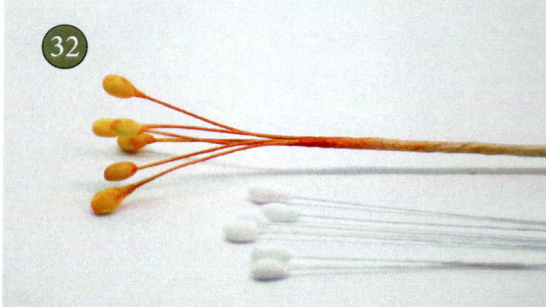

Dust the heads with Lemon Tart petal dust and dust the wires with Flame Red petal dust. Steam and allow to dry.

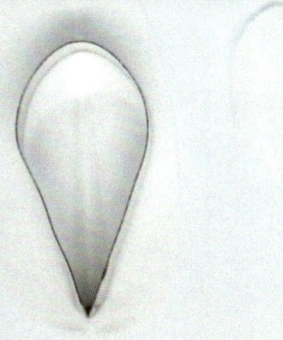

33 Roll a small amount of white sugar florist paste over the veining board. Centre the 44mm elongated rose petal cutter over the vein and cut. Insert a 26-gauge white wire into the vein groove. Use the ball tool to lightly soften the edge, then use a Cosmo petal veiner to emboss the petal.

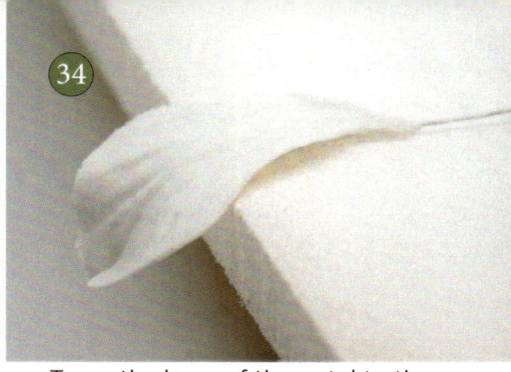

34 Taper the base of the petal to the wire. Leave to dry with the outer edge softly curled back. Repeat twice more and leave all to fully dry.

STEAMING INSTRUCTIONS

Lightly steam leaves, berries, and flowers to fix colour dusts and to prevent dusts from transferring to cakes and other details. To steam, using a hand-held clothes steamer or a kettle, hold your sugar flower, leaves, or berries approximately 4–5" away from the steam source and move them in and out of the steam, rotating them to allow the steam to reach all surfaces. Don't hold them in the steam too long or too close, as it'll soften the sugar flower paste.

35 Dust with Lemon Tart, add shading with the Flame Red and Cherry Pie. Use a Chocolate Brown edible pen to add the dark spot markings. Steam all 3 petals and allow to dry.

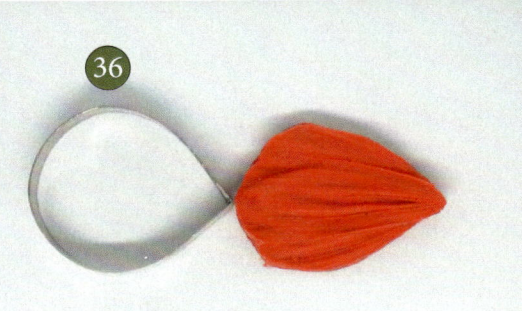

36 Prep the next set of petals using the same technique but using the 46mm rose petal. Insert a 26-gauge white wire into the vein groove. Use the ball tool to soften the edges

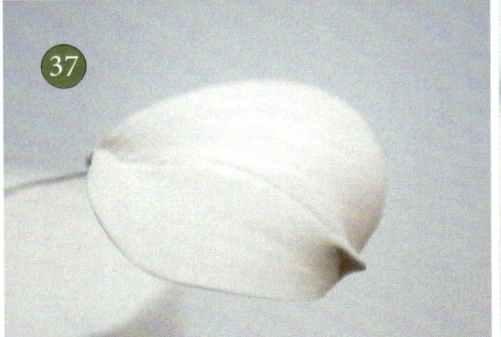

37 Emboss each petal with the petal veiner. Pinch the centres of the petal's edges and dry in a backwards curve. Once dry, dust Lemon Tart to the edges and dust over the centres.

38 Use the Flame Red and Cherry Pie dusts to add depth and definition. Add a touch of Spring Green to the tip of the pinched edge of the petals. Steam all 3 petals and allow to dry.

Cut a medium-sized calyx and soften the edges with the ball tool on the foam pad.

Add the calyx to the alstroemeria and allow to dry before dusting with Spring Green and Foliage Green. Then lightly steam the calyx and allow to dry.

Assemble the 3 smaller petals with the markings around the stamen and secure them with a little green floral tape. Then add the 3 outer petals and secure them by taping them to the end of the wire.

Berries

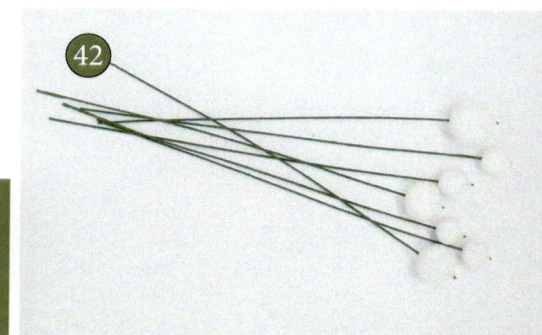

Roll small balls of white sugar florist paste. Dip a 28-gauge green wire into edible glue, remove any excess, and insert into the ball, extending out the end for its 'stalk'. Repeat for all and dry.

43

44

Roll larger balls of burgundy paste. Attach them to 26-gauge green wires using the same method as before.

Dust the small white berries with Pink Candy and Spring Green. Dust the larger burgundy berries with Claret, Aubergine, and Blackcurrant. Steam all the berries and leave to dry. Once dry, paint the larger berries with edible glaze to shine.

Leaves

45

To create the leaves use rose leaf cutters, 2 dahlia petal cutters, a calyx cutter, and a leaf veiner.

46

47

48

Roll a small amount of green sugar florist paste over the veining board. Cut a rose leaf and insert a 26-gauge green wire.

Emboss the leaves using the leaf veiner, then pinch at the base of the leaf to secure, and leave to dry. Repeat for multiple rose leaves in different sizes.

Once dry, dust with Raw Amber, a selection of greens (Spring Green, Olive, Foliage Green, and Autumn Green), and Claret. Steam and allow to dry.

49

Roll green sugar flower paste to approximately 2–3mm thick. Cut a medium calyx shape and, using the X-Acto® knife, cut into 5 leaves.

50

Insert a 28-gauge green wire into each leaf to about a third of the way up. Use the Dresden tool to add a centre vein and then pinch at the base to secure.

51

Repeat using the Dahlia petal cutters to form larger leaves. Create as many leaves as you require, plus spares in case of breakages.

52

Once dry, dust with Olive and Autumn Green, steam, and allow to dry.

53

Tape the wire of each leaf, keeping tension on the floral tape so that it sticks.

54

Arrange the leaves into small sprigs and branches by taping them together.

55

Once all flowers, foliage, and berries are complete, create an arrangement and tape together. Let the way they sit together naturally guide the shape and formation of the arrangement. If you try to force the flowers, they will break or look unnatural.

Make the wires food safe by inserting them into a straw, a posy pick, or coating them in safety seal. Once the wires are food safe, you can add them to your stacked cake.

Ellen Redmond

Splendor — Cakes and more — Bray, County Wicklow

Hailing from a small village in Bavaria, I grew up baking with my mum. She taught me how to bake with fresh yeast, which is still one of my favourite doughs, probably because the time-consuming ritual reminds me so much of home.

I fell into cake decorating by coincidence, or as my family likes to think, by accident as it has taken over my life. In 2012, I picked up a flyer about the Dublin Sugarcraft Show in my local fabric shop. I decided to enter a cake into the competition, won gold in the beginner category, and was hooked. I always loved pottery, sculpting, and painting. Sugarcraft lets me combine being a foodie with my artistic side. Having three children, I weave my cake business around my family life, and I love that I make so many friends along the way.

I fell for my handsome Irish husband in a pub in Kilkenny while on a trip around Ireland. He was travelling with a bunch of American friends on their own 'Quest for Craic'. What followed was a long-distance courtship with daily faxes(!), nightly phone calls, and lots of airmiles accumulated between Munich and Boston, where he lived at the time. Before I knew it, I left Germany and an exciting career in advertising and media behind to follow my heart to Boston.

In 2000, it was time for us to return to Ireland and settle down in the beautiful seaside town of Bray, just south of Dublin. I love our life here in the Garden County of Ireland, surrounded by natural and historic beauty and with the Wicklow Mountains on our doorstep.

Old Bray Sea Baths, Bray, County Wicklow
Photograph by Sonja Kroll | Imagewerk

nippon
MULTIDIMENSIONAL
SUGARWORK
by Ellen Redmond

EQUIPMENT AND SUPPLIES

	6x6" round dummy or cake *covered in*	Cream petal dust	Non-stick board
		Blue petal dust	Pasta roller (optional)
		Black petal dust	Small rolling pin
750g/27oz	White sugarpaste *and dried 6–24 hours*	Brown petal dust	Scalpel/X-Acto® cutter/sharp knife
		Beige petal dust	PME Dresden Tool
	7x2" round dummy		PME five-petal flower plunger cutters
300g/10oz	White modelling paste *(Saracino)*	Ethanol/Isopropyl/Dipping solution	Foam pad
		Confectioner's glaze	PME ball tool
30g /1oz	Red sugarpaste	HB pencil	Small straw *or protector cap of a paintbrush*
30g /1oz	Yellow sugarpaste	Soft pencil (min. 2B)	
500g/17.5oz	Black sugarpaste	Eraser	Sunflower Sugarart small and medium rose calyx/jasmine cutter
	White Parchment paper *(unwaxed)*	CelStick	
		Paper scissors	Quilting ruler *or 'Geodreieck' (special European set (square))*
3x	White printer paper	Small scissors	
	Small quantity of white royal icing *(piping or 15sec consistency.)*	Cello tape	Piping bag
		6mm diameter CelStick	PME 1 tip and coupler
		Paint palette	Round cutters, 4–5 ranging in size from 1.5cm–3 cm
6-10	White micro stamen *cut to 1.5cm length.*	Small spatula	
		Makeup sponge	Small green cutting mat *with 1cm gridlines*
		Paintbrush, medium, rounded flat head	Smoother
		Cotton buds	Flat head brush for glaze
		Large rolling pin	

DESIGN IDEAS, COLOUR PALETTE, AND EXECUTION

I had an idea to translate Japanese filigree wood carvings and rice paper paintings into cake. For this tutorial, I chose Japanese elements of cherry blossoms, cranes, lotus flowers, the red sun, and mountainous landscapes.

The book *Color INSPIRATIONS* by Darius A. Monsef, the founder of www.COLOURlovers.com, is a fabulous offline source to find innovative colour palettes. To determine the colour palette, use web tools such as www.COLOURlovers.com or www.design-seeds.com.

Working from background to the foreground to create depth:
A mottled, sponged sky
Mountain range silhouette, rolled paste, layered
Water, textured paste
Cherry blossom, modelled and royal-iced branches and twigs, 3D flowers, and buds in different sizes
Cranes, 2D but textured, wings 3D
Lotus, 3D, off cake extension onto base

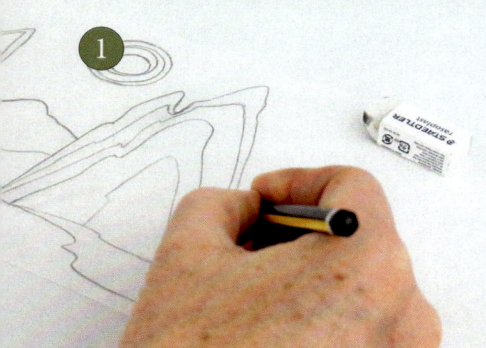

Cut a strip of parchment paper to the size of the cake's circumference. Using HB pencil, lightly draw the landscape template outlines.

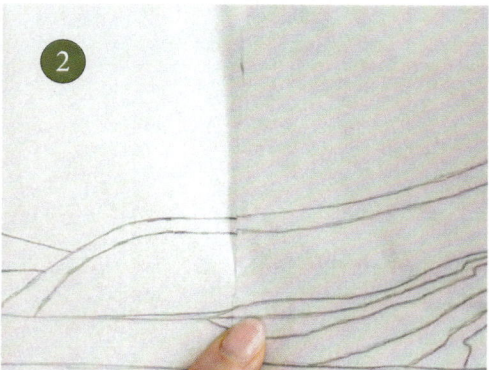

Remember, if your design wraps around the whole cake, the lines must meet.

Once you're happy with the look, go over every line in a soft pencil (2B or softer).

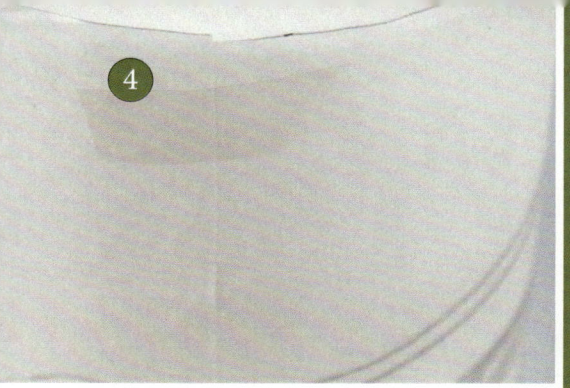

④

Attach your template to your cake pencil-side down, securing it in place with cello tape.

Tip!

If you don't want to transfer a mirror image of your template onto your cake, turn the template over after drawing the outlines in HB pencil and follow the lines with a soft pencil on that side (the side facing the cake later).

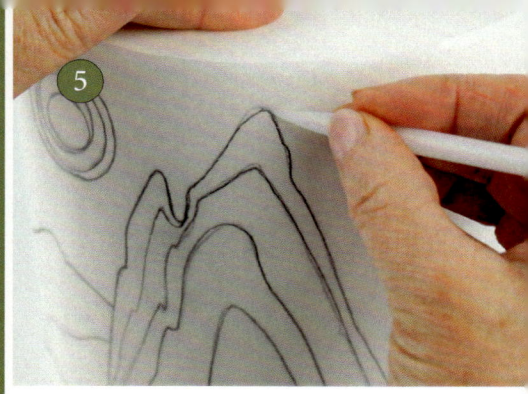

⑤

Trace the lines with enough pressure for the pencil lines to rub onto the cake without tearing the paper or digging in to the icing.

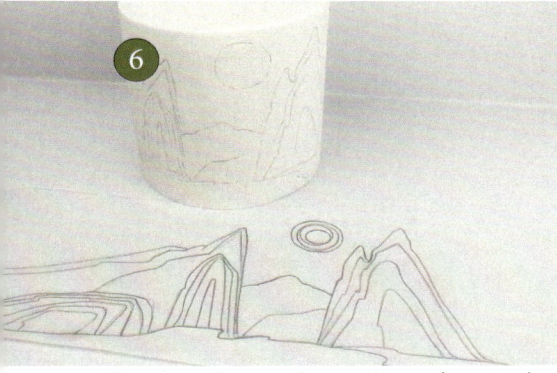

⑥

Remove the parchment template and make sure all your lines transferred. Fill in any gaps.

Tip!

Don't worry about the pencil marks on the cake. Graphite is non-toxic, and the transferred amount is negligible.

⑦

With a small spatula or the tip of a knife, transfer a small amount of each petal dust onto a paint palette or white plate.

8

Add a drop of water to each dust colour to make a paste. Dry dust mixes better with water than with the clear alcohol.

9

10

On a scrap piece of white sugarpaste, try out your colours. Sponge the colours and blend them as you would on the cake.

Mix the pastes with the paintbrush and add a squirt of clear alcohol. Using mainly alcohol prevents the liquid colour from 'eating' into the sugarpaste because it evaporates more quickly than water.

11

Dab, smudge, and layer the shades. If the colour is too opaque, load the sponge with alcohol. Have lighter and darker areas, but keep the colour semi-translucent.

12

Now move on to the cake. Sponge on a light shade of beige where the sky extends behind the mountains and the top of the cake.

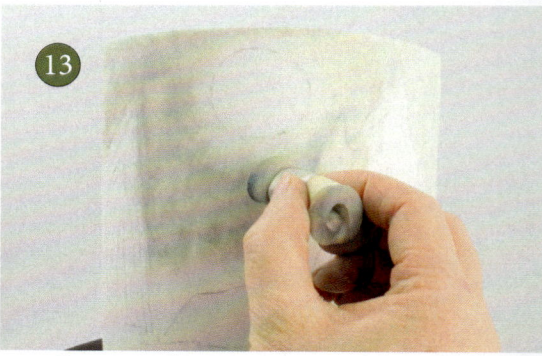

13

Once you layer on more colours, leave a lighter rim around the sun and a darker shade around the mountain edges.

Tip!

If you need to lighten an area, moisten a cotton bud with a tiny amount of water and remove any excess paint. Immediately blot with the dry end of the cotton bud to prevent the water from eating into the sugarpaste.

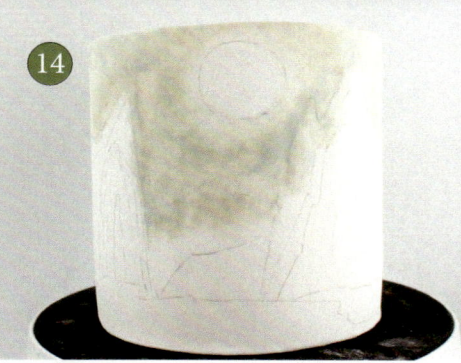

For the middle mountain that is furthest away, leave the edge around it lighter to create the illusion of the sun hitting it in the distance.

Using the same transferring technique, copy the landscape template onto white printer paper. There should be enough graphite left on your lines.

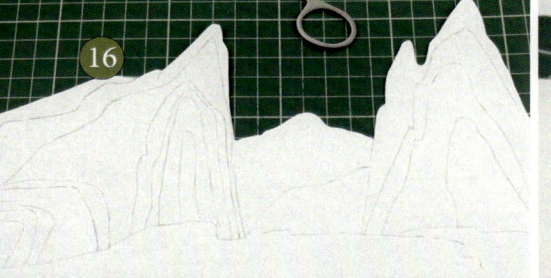

With a pair of small scissors, cut out the first silhouette outline (the one that's furthest away) from your printer paper.

Use your paper cutout as a template to cut the mountains from the white modelling paste layer by layer.

Roll out white modelling paste to about 0.5mm (or #5 KitchenAid® pasta roller). Leave the modelling paste to firm up a little, just enough that it's easier to cut without dragging and keeps its shape when lifted (this depends on humidity and temperature).

Use the previous paper cutoff to position the next layer.

Keep building those layers.

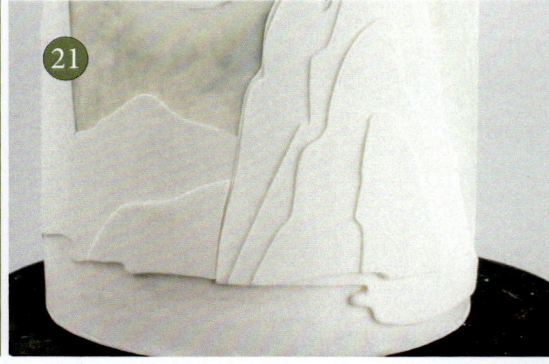

Brush the back of the mountains with water and transfer the mountains to the cake, matching it up to the pencil outline

Roll some modelling paste to the same thickness as the layered mountains. Cut out the corresponding lake piece from the paper template and use this piece to cut the lake out of modelling paste.

Use your Dresden tool to create the wavy water texture. When adding the texture, reduce the waves in size the further back you go.

Roll some white modelling paste to about 1mm. With the PME five-petal flower plunger cutters, cut cherry blossoms in the 3 smallest sizes.

25 Transfer the blossoms to a foam pad and thin the edges of the blossoms (big end) and cup them (small end) with a ball tool.

26 Roll tiny balls of modelling paste in a few different sizes (1mm–5mm) as cherry blossom buds.

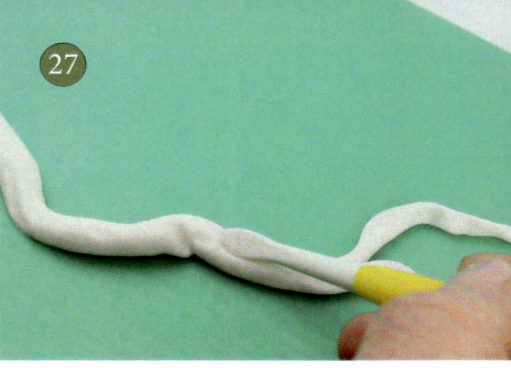

27 Roll some tapered sausages of modelling paste up to 2cm thick. Form irregular zigzag bends and add ridges for gnarly branches.

28 Attach the gnarly branches to the cake with some royal icing. The royal icing should be soft piping consistency. (Some call it '15sec' icing after the time it takes for drips or cuts in your royal icing to blend back together in the bowl).

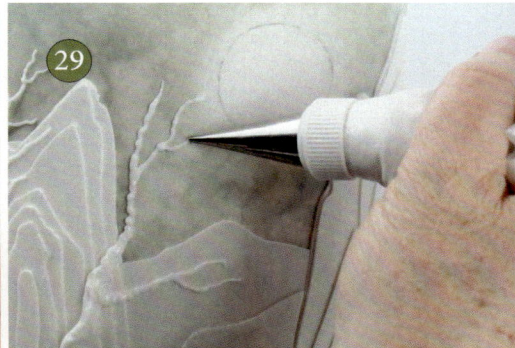

29 Extend the branches into finer twigs with royal icing. Control the thickness by using more or less pressure on the piping bag.

 **Tip!**

If you pipe a line or something that you regret, don't worry. You can easily remove mistakes with a damp paintbrush.

30

Add the blossoms. You can add finer twigs when you put on the smallest buds at the ends of the twigs.

31

Attach the blossoms and buds with small dots of royal icing. Use small blossoms at the ends of the branches. Pick up and place tiny pieces with a damp paintbrush.

32

LEAVE OUT THIS STEP IF THIS CAKE TIER WILL BE EATEN!

Pipe small royal icing dots into the larger flowers. While the royal icing is soft, place 2 micro stamens (cut to 1.5cm length) into each flower centre.

33

Finish piping the centres of all the blossoms. Add the last of the very fine twiggy ends and some tiny royal icing dots for the smallest of buds. These dots don't need to be attached to the twigs. Let them hover, and it will give the tree a delicate look.

34

Sketch the cranes on white paper or use the template provided.

35

Cut out the crane templates with a small pair of scissors.

36 Roll some modelling paste to about 3mm and place your crane templates on top. Cut out the cranes with a blade.

37

38 Roll modelling paste to 2mm and cut a separate wing from it. Transfer the wing to the foam pad and curl and texture the wing as before.

Transfer the cranes to a foam pad. Use modelling tools to add dimension and texture. Make sure the paste hasn't dried up. Use a ball tool to thin and cup the wing feathers. With the ball tool half on the edge of the feather end and half on the pad, run from the outer edge of the feather inwards to curl up the feather. Use the Dresden tool to add more texture to the eye and beak line.

39 Attach the wing to the crane with a bit of water.

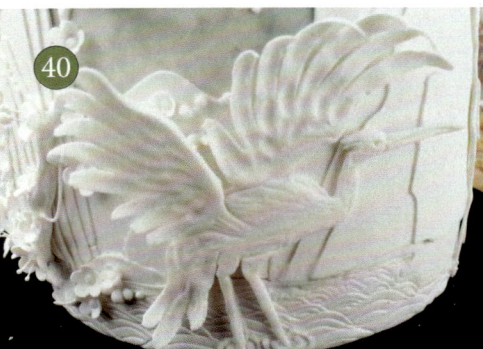

40 Moisten the backs of the cranes and stick them to the side of the cake. You can pipe a water ripple around their legs where they stand in the water.

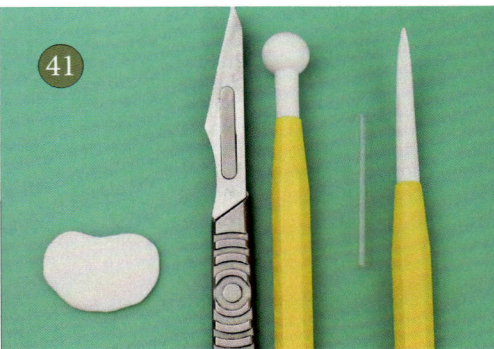

41 Roll modelling paste to 1mm and cut out a few freeform lotus leaves in different sizes.

42

Cup the lotus leaves with the ball tool, slightly off centre, near the leaves' indents.

43

Use a small straw or the protective cover of a small paintbrush to make the centre for the lotus leaves.

44

Use your Dresden tool to texture and vein your lotus leaves.

45

Use the dull end of the CelStick to frill the edge of the lotus leaves and bend them upwards.

47

Use the big end of your ball tool to thin and cup the flowers.

46

Roll out modeling paste to 1mm. Use rose calyx cutters for your lotus flowers; cut them in 2 sizes.

48

Roll a small piece of modelling paste into a little ball (2–3mm) for the lotus centre. Place the ball on the tip of your CelStick and use the scalpel to make tiny cuts all around.

49

To assemble the lotus flower, put 1 of the cupped flowers inside the other, sticking them with a little water. Place them so that the petals alternate. Attach the centre again with a little water.

50

Before you attach the flowers and leaves, shape them to look right. For example, the flowers on the side of the cake need to be flattened a bit. Attach the flowers to the cake with royal icing and leave some aside to 'spill over' onto the base tier.

51

For the ombre shades of the sun, take yellow and red sugarpaste/ modelling paste and 4–5 different-sized circle cutters ranging from 3cm–1.5 cm.

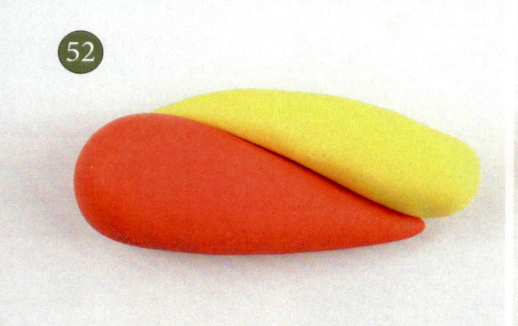

52

Roll the 2 balls of sugarpaste into teardrop shapes and place them 'head to toe'. If the paste is warm, you won't need water.

53

Roll the 'head to toe' bonded teardrops into a sausage.

54

Cut the two-tone sausage into 4 equal pieces.

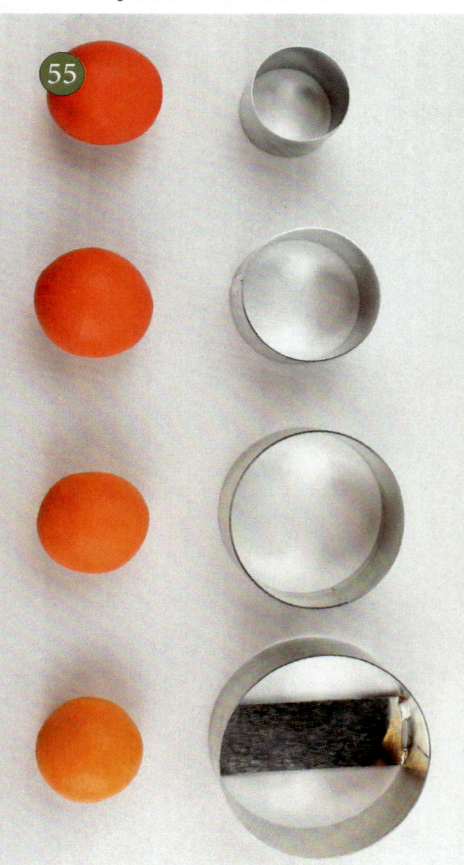

55

Knead and blend the 2 colours together in each piece and roll them into balls.

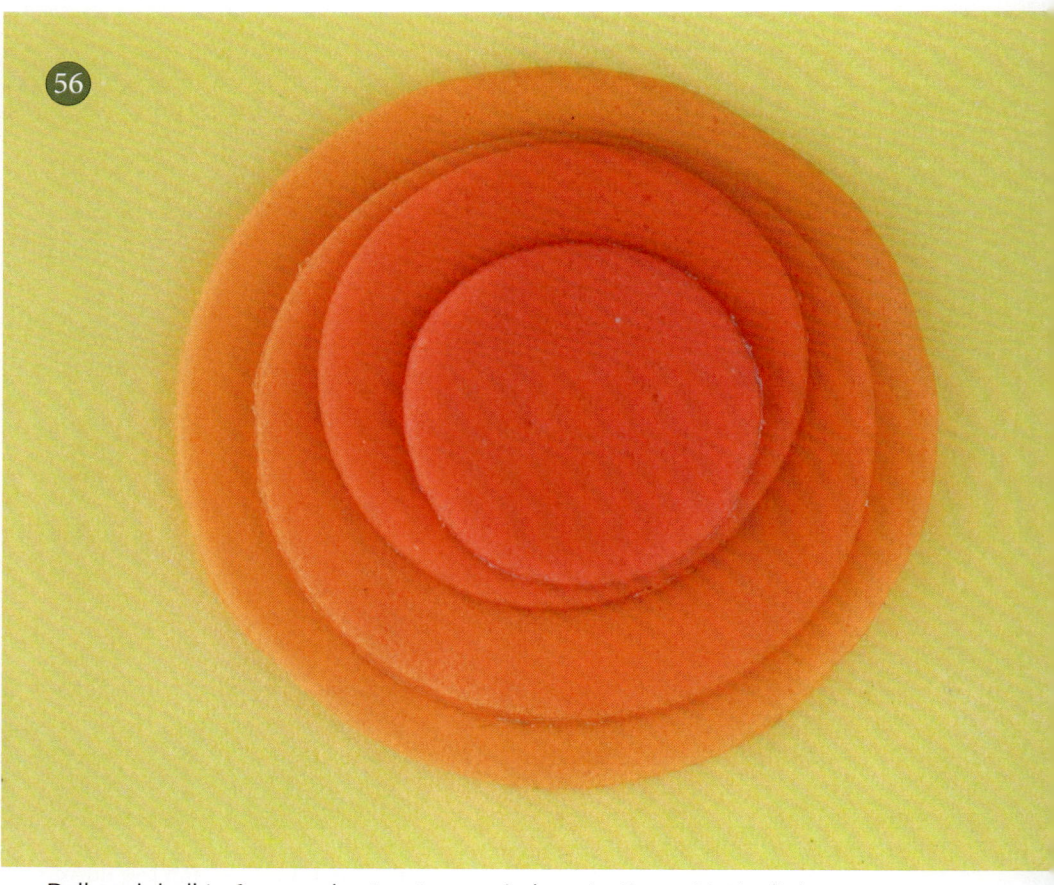

56

Roll each ball to 1mm and cut out your circles, starting with the lightest orange as the biggest circle. Glue the circles on top of each other with a little water.

57

Brush the back of the sun lightly with water and transfer it onto the cake.

58

Cover and smooth the top of the base tier with black sugarpaste.

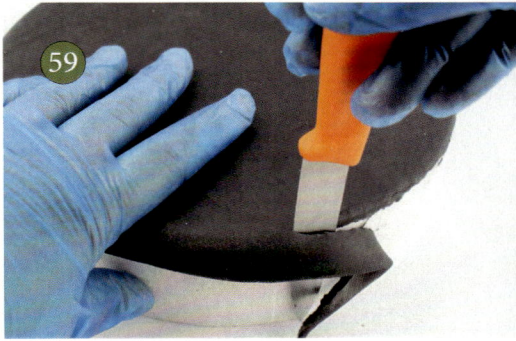

59

With a sharp knife, trim off the excess paste. Hold your knife at a 90° angle and stay close to the edge to get a neat trim.

60

The widths of your trim strips depend on the thickness of your paste on top. Measure the total height of your tier, including the paste on top. Take away 4cm from that tier and divide the remainder by 2, which will give you the width of 1 trim. For example, total height of tier: 5.4cm minus 4cm = 1.4cm divided by 2 = 7mm width per trim. Roll a long piece of black sugarpaste to 4mm. Use a long quilting ruler or 'Geodreieck' as a guide for cutting your trim strips to the width you worked out.

61

IMPORTANT:
This job requires precision or your 'puzzle pieces' won't match up.

Cut the T-shapes on a cutting mat with 1cm gridlines. Roll black sugarpaste to 4mm and 2mm. Use the template provided or the gridlines on your mat as a guide to cut the T-shapes in the 2 different thicknesses.

62

Apply the 2 trim strips with a little water to the top and bottom of the base. Keep a 4cm clearance between them to fit your T-shapes. Brush each T-shape with water and attach them in the pattern shown to the base.

63

Place the completely covered base on top of a food can on your turntable. Use confectioner's glaze and a medium, flat, rounded paintbrush to gloss the base to give a lacquered look. Put on at least 3–4 coats. Make sure to leave time for each coat to dry before adding the next. Once the base has dried, fit the top tier to the base with a dollop of royal icing. Finally, add the lotus leaves and flowers that you saved to 'spill' onto the base.

Use these templates as a general guide to recreate the effects shown in this tutorial. Photocopy the templates to a percentage that suits your own cake size. Or create your own landscape using these templates as inspiration.

A SEASIDE
wedding
by Corinna Maguire

EQUIPMENT AND SUPPLIES

7"/18cm wide	Square cake *(1.5"/4cm tall)* *For cutting the lighthouse pieces*	5tbsp	Buttercream		2.75"/7cm	Circle cutter
		3x	Cake card *(4"/10cm)*		3.5"/8cm	Circle cutter
		1x	Cake card *(7"/18cm)*		3.75"/9cm	Circle cutter
7"/18cm wide	Round cake *(5"/12.5cm tall)* *Rope tier*	1x	Cake drum *(10"/25cm)*			
		8x	Cake dowels *Plastic 8"/20cm*		*Petal dusts*	
10"/18cm wide	Round cake *(5"/12.5cm tall)* *Waves tier*		Edible glaze spray *(Dinkydoodle)*		Grey mist	
					Toasted almond	
200g/7oz	Beige fondant *mixed with*	2	Gelatin sheets *(4.5" x 3"/11cm x 7.5cm)*		Natural midnight blue *(Roxy & Rich)*	
200g/7oz	White modelling chocolate	1	Wafer paper sheet		Nature navy blue *(Roxy & Rich)*	
		6x	Acetate sheets			
300g/10oz	Beige fondant	1x	Palette knife		*Brushes*	
420g/15oz	White fondant	1x	Rolling pin		Medium fluffy brush	
500g/18oz	Light blue fondant	1x	X-Acto® blade		Small detail brush	
	Ganache *(150g white chocolate and 60ml double cream)*	1x	Extruder		Medium flat brush	
		1x	Large shamrock attachment			
		1x	Small rectangle attachment			
		1x	Set of modelling tools			
		1x	Paper edge pattern cutter			

1

To make the centre tier, ice and cover your cake with a light brown fondant. Sharp edges aren't necessary.

2

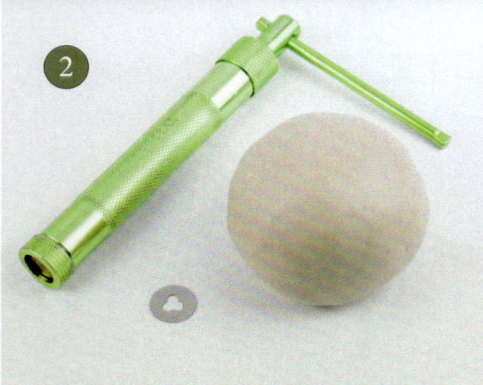

Mix 50% modelling chocolate with 50% fondant in the same shade of brown. Get an extruder and a large shamrock bit.

3

Using the shamrock attachment, extrude a full piece of the 50/50 mix. To give the appearance of rope, twist it in 1 direction.

4

Starting at the base, attach the rope to the fondant. You may need a little water to secure it.

5

6

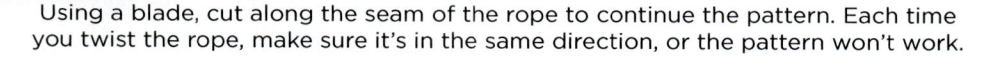

Secure the pieces together with a little water.

Using a blade, cut along the seam of the rope to continue the pattern. Each time you twist the rope, make sure it's in the same direction, or the pattern won't work.

7

To see how far to wrap the rope around the top, place the 4" cake board for the top lighthouse tier onto the centre of the rope tier.

8

Using a dry brush, take some petal dust a shade darker than the rope dust and brush it onto a piece of tissue paper until it's almost gone.

9

To give the rope more depth, brush the remaining dust into the creases between the ropes.

Edible Glue

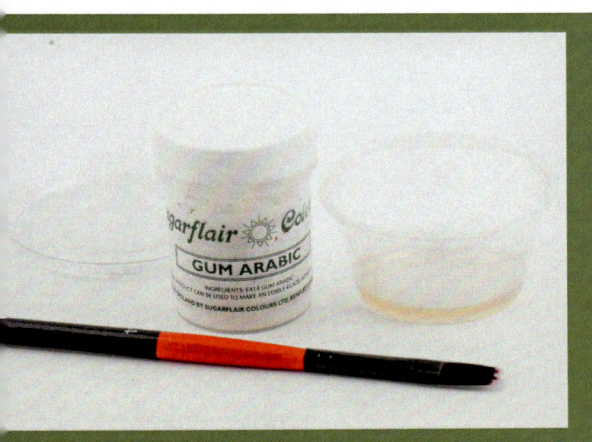

I normally only use water or vodka when attaching cake pieces together. Edible glue comes in handy when gravity is working against you, if a piece is very heavy, or if there's structure involved. We'll be using edible glue for this tutorial. Some cake shops supply pots of edible glue, but you can also make your own using this recipe.

YOU WILL NEED:

1 tbsp   gum arabic
2 tbsp   warm water

Mix the gum arabic with warm water until it's completely dissolved. Store the mixture in the fridge in an airtight container. (Discard after 6 weeks.)

10 For the Celtic heart knot, bend a length of twisted rope at a 45° angle and loop each end back on itself into a heart shape.

11 Cut off the excess rope, wrapping the left side around and under the edge. Tuck the right side underneath the overlapping edge.

12 Cut a piece of rope long enough to fit under the heart's top left corner and around the outside of the bottom right edge.

13 Weave another length of rope under the upper right piece and over the central piece. Tuck and attach this piece to look as though it joins up with the piece that's wound around the left-hand side.

14 Push any loose pieces into place and secure them with some water if needed. Re-mark any lines that rubbed off. Leave this heart to harden before placing it on the cake.

Tip!

Smaller pieces of modelling chocolate can melt quickly. Before working, cool your hands with an ice pack and towel them dry and use your tools as much as possible.

(15)

Once the heart is solid enough to handle, attach it to the top section of the rope tier with a little vodka or edible glue.

(16)

To give the heart depth and to make it easier to see on the rope stack, when the heart has dried into place, dust around its edges as before.

(17)

Extrude another long piece of rope and cut it in half.

(18)

Pull the top left section of heart up a little and insert 1 of the pieces of rope underneath. Secure with some vodka or edible glue.

(19)

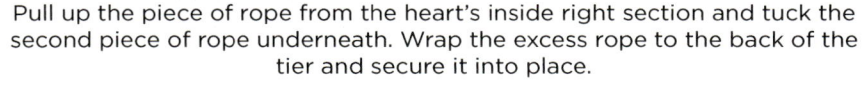

(20)

Cut the ends of the excess rope to a point and tuck them in to a seam to make it look as though the rope is coming from somewhere.

Pull up the piece of rope from the heart's inside right section and tuck the second piece of rope underneath. Wrap the excess rope to the back of the tier and secure it into place.

21

To help the pattern pop and make it more visible, dust all of the deeper sections of the Celtic heart knot.

22

23

Cut a small hole in the centre of the 4" cake board and get 2.75" (7cm), 3.25" (8cm), and 3.75" (9cm) circle cutters.

If you've dusted any section too much, wipe away the surface using a paper towel and some vodka. This technique leaves the dusted areas in the deeper sections. Now you're 1 tier down with 2 to go!

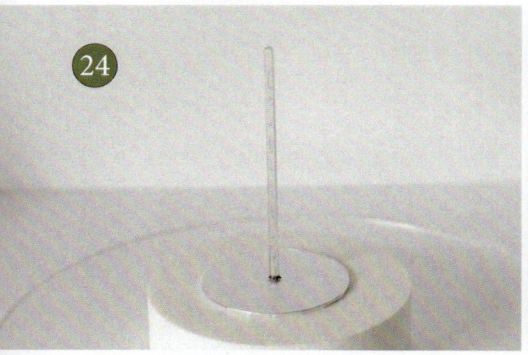

24

To support the cake, place the cake board onto a cake dummy and insert the dowel through the hole and into the dummy.

25

Cover a 4" cake board in buttercream. Cut a piece of cake using the largest circle cutter and place it on the board. Layer with more buttercream.

26

Using the 3.25" (8cm) circle cutter, cut 2 pieces of cake, and layer the pieces, stacking them.

27 Finally, using the 2.75" (7cm) circle cutter, cut another piece of cake. Your final stacked cake should be around 6" (15cm) tall.

28 Carve off any edges that are sticking out. Try to get a nice, smooth, slightly tapered tower. Push in the dowel so that it's almost flush with the top of the cake.

29 Cover the drum with wax paper and coat the tower with some white chocolate ganache. A flexi smoother can come in handy here.

30 Place the 'ganached' cake in the fridge to set fully. Remove the wax paper.

32 Roll out a panel of white fondant, tall and long enough to wrap around the sides. Dust with corn flour and roll up. Unroll the fondant, keeping the base of the fondant flush with the bottom.

31 Lightly moisten the top of the tower and cover it with a circle of fondant similar in size to the top. Cut off the excess around the edges. Make sure the cake top is level.

33 Smooth down any lumps and bumps. Use an acupuncture needle or a pin to remove any air bubbles.

34 Cut through the 2 layers of the fondant overlap.

35 Peel back the top layer and remove the excess fondant from underneath. Replace the top layer so that it's flush with the lower layer.

36 Using a flexi smoother, smooth away the seam.

37 Cut off the excess fondant at the top and blend in the top seam.

38 Before the fondant dries, using a small flat tool such as a sugar shaper, create small rectangular windows by pushing in the fondant slightly.

39 Cut 4 strips of wafer paper 0.25" (.75cm) wide and at least 3" (7.5cm) long.

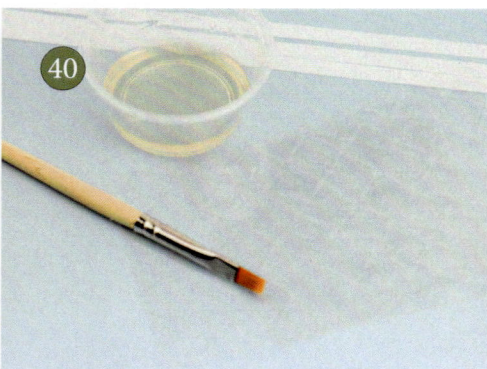

40 Get 2 sheets of leaf gelatin, some edible glue, and a small flat paintbrush.

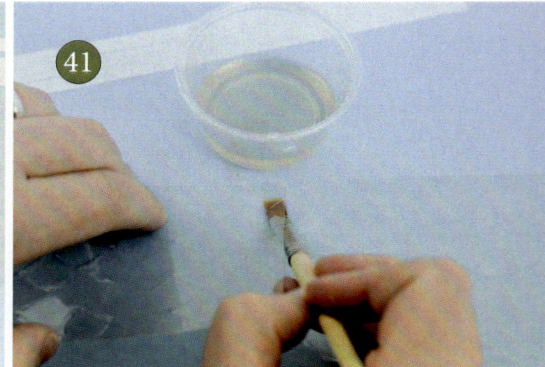

41 Paint a strip of edible glue down the short side of the gelatin sheet and place the second sheet overtop, overlapping it by about 0.25" (.6cm).

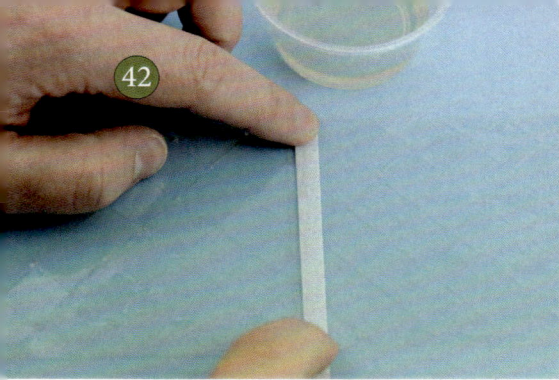

42

To give extra support to the seam, paint another strip of edible glue onto the seam and place 1 of the strips of wafer paper on top.

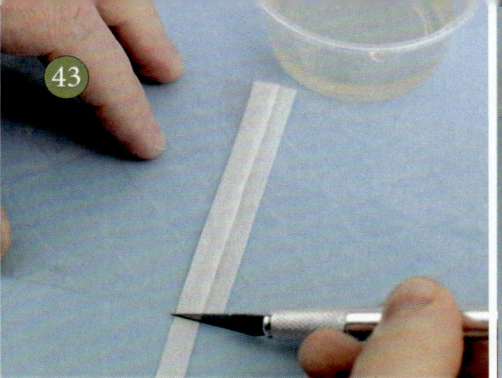

43

To support both sides of the gelatin sheets, flip over the joined sheets and repeat this process. Cut off any excess wafer paper at the edge. Leave to dry.

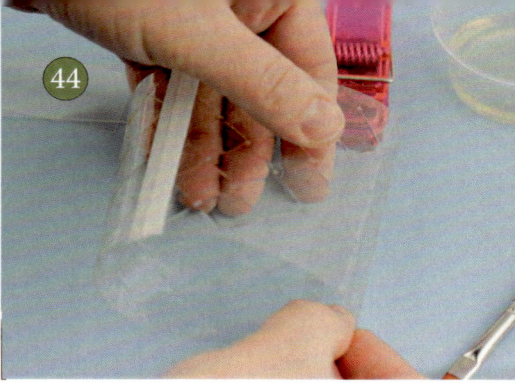

44

Once fully dry, roll the gelatin sheets into a tube and glue the overlap, holding it together tightly. This process can be a bit finicky.

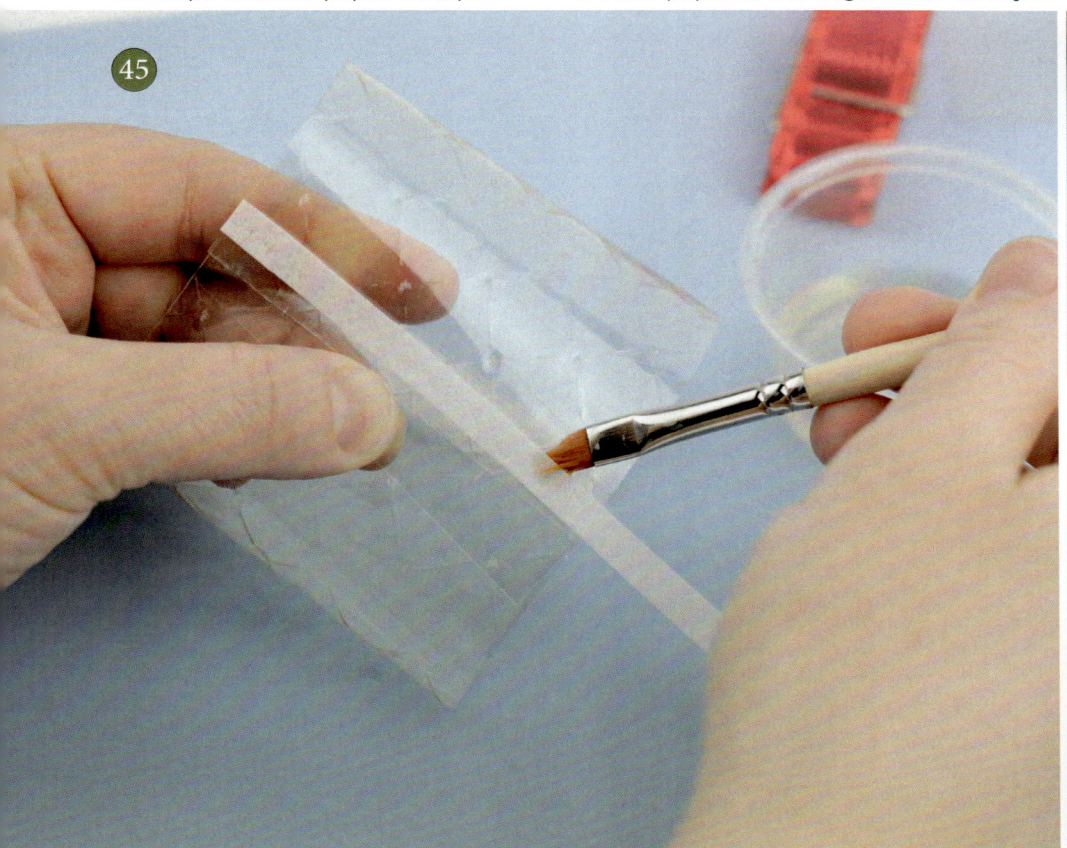

45

Holding the newly glued pieces together, attach a strip of wafer paper to the tube's outside seam with edible glue.

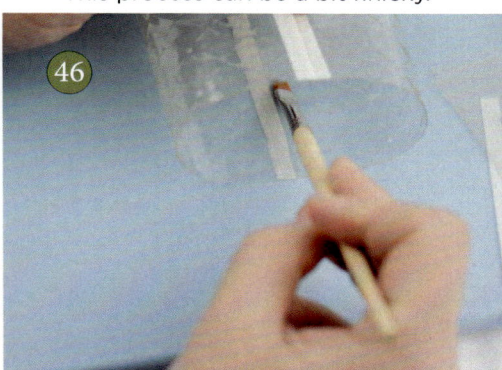

46

Glue and add a second strip to the inside of the tube.

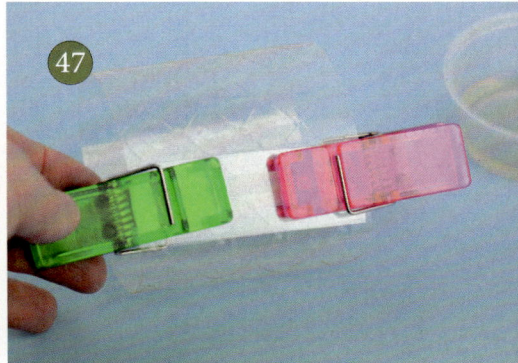

47

To keep this seam tightly together until it's fully dry, use 2 flat clips. (I'm sure you have better things to do than holding it!)

48

Using 2 dowels as a height level, roll out some light blue fondant large enough to cover the top of the tower. Glue into place and cut off the excess.

49

Cover a 4" round cake board on the top and bottom using edible glue to secure it. Glue it to the top of the tower. Make sure it's perfectly centred.

50

Use a level bar to make sure that the top of the cake isn't leaning. If it isn't level, press down or add extra fondant under the cake board.

51

52

Using the extruder and a thin rectangle attachment, extrude light blue for the outside of the cake board.

Centre the leaf gelatin glass onto the cake board. Push it into the fondant and secure it into place with a little edible glue.

53

Paint edible glue around the outside edge of the cake board and secure the blue strip into place.

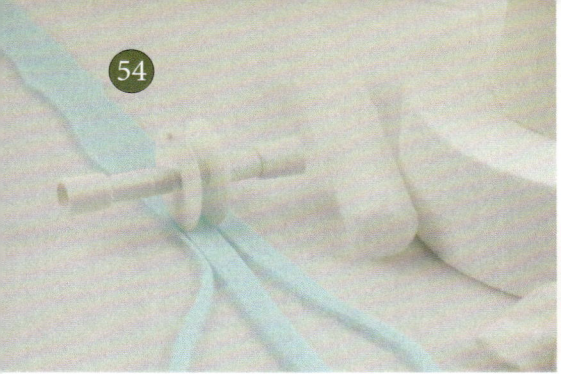

54 Using a ribbon cutter, cut a strip approximately 0.5in (1.25cm) in width.

55 Attach this blue ribbon underneath the cake card using edible glue to keep it in place.

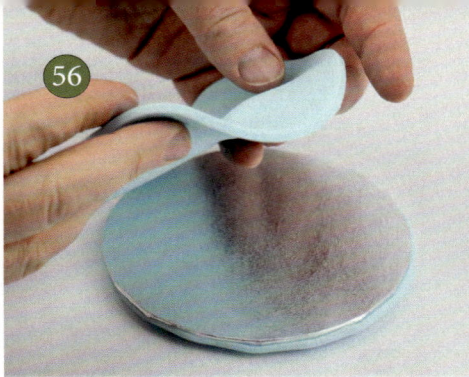

56 Cover a second cake board with more of the blue fondant on both sides, securing with edible glue.

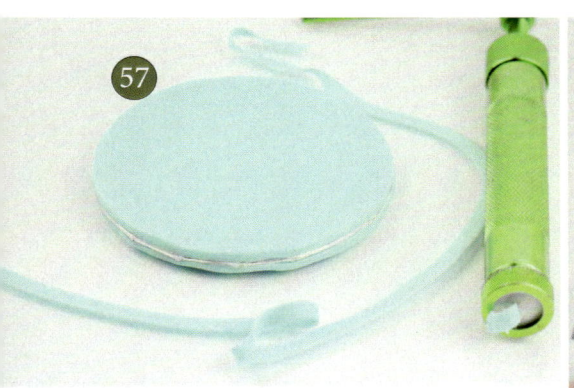

57 Cover the edges with another strip of blue fondant, securing with edible glue. Leave to dry.

59 Using a ruler or straight edge, cut out a 1" width of the designed edge of wafer paper.

58 To create the railing on the lighthouse, use a paper edge cutter press to make an interesting design on the edge of a full sheet of edible wafer paper.

60

Paint a little strip of edible glue onto the bottom rim of the gelatin glass and wrap it with the detailed wafer paper strip.

61

To create a half sphere for the top of the lighthouse, use a plastic dome mould dusted with corn flour and push in blue fondant. Leave to harden.

62

Using edible glue, place the dome onto the dried, double-sided blue cake board.

63

To hide any seams, extrude some white fondant and, using edible glue, wrap it around the base of the dome

64

To create a little detail for the top of the lighthouse, find a smaller dome shape (I used my paint palette).

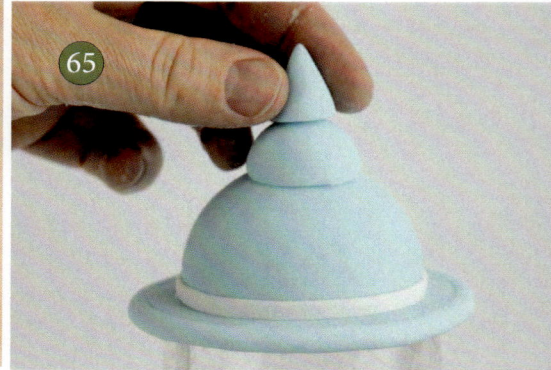

65

Finally, using a little more edible glue, add a little cone shape for the very top. Have some fun with this part.

66 Add another wafer paper railing to the exterior of the bottom cake board. Secure the railing into place with the edible glue and hold until it sticks.

67 Place a circle of wax paper onto the base of the gelatin glass.

68 Insert a battery-powered tea light on top of the wax paper.

69 We have light! But turn it off until the big day to save on battery power. Now, back to work!

70 With very little dark grey petal dust on your brush, dust under the blue edge and onto the white walls.

71 Dust under the railings and in all of the creases and the corners on the lid. Remember that less is more!

Hard Gelatin Waves

It's a good idea to leave this gelatin-covered tier for last. Gelatin is a finicky material. One minute it's funky and firm, and the next minute you're dealing with a puddle on your cake. The only way that I've gotten gelatin to work when attaching it to cakes is to seal the fondant on the cake with an edible glaze spray. Gelatin tends to suck all of the moisture out of everything, so be careful and keep in mind that humidity and moisture will affect it.

2 tbsp   Gelatin powder
8 tbsp   Warm water
          Food colouring gel

In a bowl, mix together the gelatin powder, warm water, and your food colouring. You can use food colouring gel or petal dusts. The dusts may not disintegrate fully, although I like this effect.

Microwave the mix in bursts of no more than 30 seconds and stir until fully combined. The colour may alter slightly—go with it.

Normally at this point, you would scrape off the foam, but we're creating sea waves, so a little sea foam is okay.

Pour strips of the gelatin onto acetate sheets. Allow to fully dry before attaching the waves to the glazed fondant on the cake.

Select a couple of shades of blue to mix with your gelatin powder mix.

Add in the water and put in a little light blue colour (either dusts or gels). You will increase the shade of blue in later batches.

Microwave the mix and stir until fully combined and until the gelatin completely disintegrates.

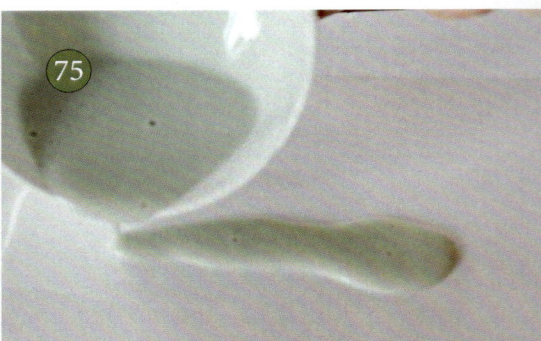

Pour out strips of gelatin onto acetate sheets.

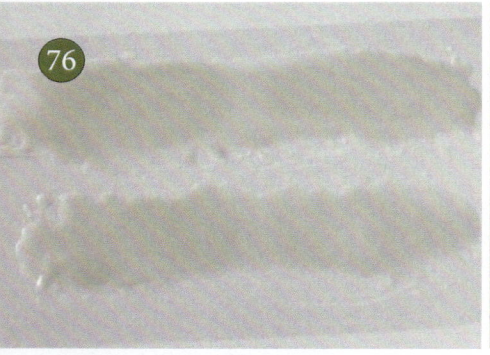

Spread out the gelatin before it starts to dry. Make 2 strips of gelatin per acetate sheet.

Add more blue colouring to the gelatin to deepen the shade. Repeat for a third, darker shade.

78 Stick the acetate sheets together and wrap them around a dummy or cake tin similar in size to the actual cake.

79 Allow to fully dry overnight (depending on humidity). The gelatin should be completely dry, falling off the acetate, and not tacky to the touch.

80 Cover your cake drum with a light brown fondant. Cover the cake with a light blue fondant similar to the gelatin. Sharp edges aren't necessary here.

81 Once all of the gelatin strips are fully dry, place them on the cake in order of depth of colour. Place the light ones on first, and overlap them with the darker ones.

82 **IMPORTANT!** Coat the cake and cake board with an edible glaze or shellac. Spray 2 or 3 layers, allowing each layer to fully dry before spraying the next layer.

83 Cut the light and medium shades of gelatin strips in half lengthwise. These shades don't need to be a perfect line.

84

For the darker shade of blue gelatin, use a straight edge to cut these strips in a straight line. This shade will rest on the baseboard.

85

Paint a light coating of edible glue onto the cake top.

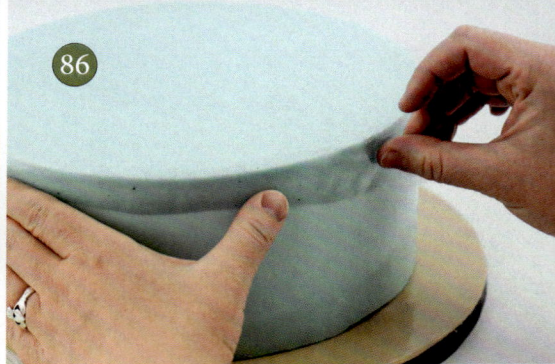

86

Attach the lightest layer of gelatin waves to the edible glue. Extend this layer over the edge if you like.

87

Overlap each layer, slowly moving to the darker shades of blue as you get lower.

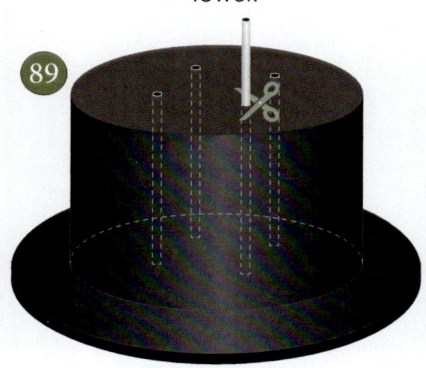

89

To support the 2 tiers above, insert 4 dowels into the base tier. Add royal icing before attaching it to secure it into place.

88

Line the straight edge of the dark blue gelatin waves so that they rest against the brown base tier.

"Never put off till tomorrow,
what you can do the day after tomorrow."
Oscar Wilde

RECIPES

Caryna Camerino

Camerino Bakery — Capel Street, Dublin

How Camerino Bakery got its name...

I started my bakery from home and sold my cakes at market stalls, all to move away from a job that I hated. (Does it get much worse than working in Human Resources for a construction firm during an economic collapse? My job was basically firing people every day). As my bakery business grew, I began supplying independent restaurants in Dublin. I had a dream to open my own boutique bakery— somewhere with a big window that I could fill with beautiful cakes.

As I dreamed of my bakery, I also dreamed of the name, and in 2014, I starting making moves. My business was registered as Lovin' from the Oven Limited.

I had been trading as Caryna's Cakes, but people seemed to struggle with the Caryna part: 'Carnya?', 'Carvna?,' 'Ca-ryena?' It's the Y that throws people. Oddly though, the website www. lovinfromtheoven.ie was taken. Unlike in America, in Ireland, you must have the company name before you can acquire the website name. I had a look at the website ... It was a cake company (no shock there). Run by a woman named Corinna. Before my company was registered, no company by that name came up on the search. As it turns out, Corinna's company registration was processed just one day before mine.

I rang Corinna to introduce myself and to explain this odd collision of similarities. She was so nice, and she was equally shocked. She asked, 'Where is your accent from?' 'Oh, I'm Canadian', I said, 'But I've been living here in Ireland for ten and a half years ... ' 'What??!! I'm Canadian too'.

So there you have it. Lovin' from the Oven is available on the East and West coasts of Ireland, brought to you by two Canadian Carynas/Corinnas who spell their names weirdly and had the bright ideas to call their bakery companies the same thing at the same time.

I'm so grateful that Corinna is so talented because if anyone ever mistakes her cakes for mine, I really benefit!

I named my bakery Camerino, my surname, which translates from Italian as 'little room'. Camerino Bakery is a tiny, award-winning spot in the middle of Dublin.

POUND CAKE

Yield: 1 x 8"/20cm round cakes
Prep time: 20 mins
Baking time: 45 mins

This cake doesn't have as much butter as a traditional pound cake; instead, it uses thick yogurt to liven up the batter. The result is a dense yet moist cake that can withstand a fondant covering. Your cake will bake to about 2" (5cm) high, so double or triple the recipe as needed.

INGREDIENTS

3 large	Free-range eggs
1 cup (330g)	Granulated sugar
1 cup (225g or 2 sticks)	Soft butter
	(I use salted, Irish butter)
³/₄ cup (210g	Thick yogurt, such as Greek
	Zest of 1 lemon
1 ¹/₂ tsp (7g)	Vanilla extract
1 ¹/₂ cups (340g)	Self-raising flour

DIRECTIONS

1. Preheat the oven to 160°C (325°F).

2. Line an 8" (20cm) round tin with parchment or baking paper.

3. Beat the eggs and sugar, butter, zest, yogurt, and vanilla until the batter is mixed.

4. Sift in the flour and stir until smooth.

5. Pour the batter into the lined tin.

6. Bake for 45 minutes. Cool for 20 minutes, then remove from the tin. Cool completely.

   Voilà!

Caryna Camerino — Camerino Bakery, 158 Capel Street, Dublin 1, Ireland — www.camerino.ie

MARBLE CAKE

Yield:	2 x 10" (25cm) round cakes
Prep time:	20 mins
Baking time:	45 mins

This cake is the best of both worlds. It has chocolate and vanilla sponge, which means it's a crowd pleaser. The buttermilk in the recipe helps keep the cake fresh for three days, which means more time for decorating. Your cake will bake to about 2" (5cm) high, so double the recipe as needed.

DIRECTIONS

1. Preheat the oven to 180°C (350°F).

2. Line a 2 x 10" (25cm) round tin with parchment or baking paper.

3. Beat the eggs and sugar, butter, and vanilla until the batter is mixed.

4. In a separate bowl, mix the eggs and buttermilk.

5. Start by adding 1/3 of your flour to the sugar and butter batter. Mix until combined. Add 1/3 of your egg and buttermilk mix. Continue to alternate the dry and wet ingredients in thirds until it's all mixed together. This is your vanilla mix.

6. In a separate large bowl, mix the cocoa and milk to form a paste. Add in half of your vanilla mix and stir until you have an even chocolate colour. This is now your chocolate mix.

7. Alternate between dropping heaped spoonfuls of vanilla and chocolate batter into the lined tins. Using a knife, cut through the batter a few times to get a swirled effect.

8. Bake for 45 minutes. Cool for 20 minutes, then remove from the tin. Cool completely.

INGREDIENTS

1 ¹/₂ cups (350g or 3 sticks)	Soft butter
	(I use salted, Irish butter)
1 tsp (5g)	Vanilla extract
1 ¹/₄ cups (370g)	Superfine or caster sugar
2 cups (450g)	Self-raising flour, sifted
1 cup (240ml)	Buttermilk
4 large	Free-range eggs
....	
¹/₂ cup (120g)	Full-fat milk
¹/₂ cup (50g)	Cocoa powder

CHOCOLATE BISCUIT CAKE

Yield:	Either a 2" (5cm) high 10" (25cm) round cake or a 3" (7.5cm) high 8" (20cm) round cake
Prep time:	40 mins
Baking time:	4 hours to set (no baking!)

This cake is Ireland's best-kept secret. It requires no baking and will stay fresh for at least 10 days. It's heavy and solid and is a favourite for fondant cakes. You can easily repair any holes or uneven bits with melted chocolate or chocolate ganache. Double the recipe as needed. If you need your cake to be tall, you can build a wall in your tin with cardboard, then line with baking paper or, even better, acetate.

INGREDIENTS

2 cups (450g or 4 sticks) Butter
(I use salted, Irish butter)

2 ¹/₂ cups (420g) 55% chocolate chips or chunks

1 ¹/₄ cups (210g) Milk chocolate chips or chunks

6 ¹/₂ cups (715g) Crushed biscuits, *such as digestive biscuits, rich tea biscuits, ginger biscuits... Ideally, the biscuit chunks are no larger than a walnut*

1/3 cup (75g) Golden syrup or corn syrup

DIRECTIONS

1. Line your tin with parchment or baking paper.

2. Melt your butter, 55% chocolate, milk chocolate, and syrup in the microwave, 1 minute at a time. Stir in between each time you put the mixture in the microwave or stir over a double boiler.

3. When all of your chocolate is melted and smooth, mix in your biscuits. Stir to coat all the biscuits well.

4. Pour your chocolate biscuit mixture into your tin. Tap the tin and bang it on your counter a few times. This will help the mixture spread into all the corners and will allow air bubbles to come up so that the top relaxes to a smoother finish.

5. Leave your cake to rest in the fridge for at least 4 hours or, preferably, overnight.

6. The cake should be at room temperature for serving or it will be too difficult to cut.

You can jazz up this cake with mini marshmallows, nuts, liquor, malted chocolate candy, raisins, etc. (Dried fruit is a controversial addition and a controversial subject among chocolate biscuit cake lovers.)

Enjoy!

Caryna Camerino — Camerino Bakery, 158 Capel Street, Dublin 1, Ireland — www.camerino.ie

GANACHE

Yield: Enough to cover and fill an 8" round cake (4" tall)
Prep time: 10 mins
Making time: 15 mins plus resting time

Ganache is a favourite cake covering for so many cake decorators, especially when dealing with sharp edges and structured cakes. Ganache gives cakes a strong, smooth surface to support the application of fondant and is a delicious addition to any cake. For a really tasty ganache, don't skimp on the quality of the chocolate! To alter the flavours and complement your cake flavours, add liquors or concentrated liquid food flavourings.

INGREDIENTS

DARK CHOCOLATE GANACHE

750g (30oz)   **Dark chocolate**
(with at least 55% cocoa solids)

375ml (15fl oz)   **Double cream**
(heavy cream with at least 35% fat)

WHITE CHOCOLATE GANACHE

825g (30oz)   **White chocolate**
(with at least 20% cocoa solids)

330ml (12fl oz)   **Double cream**
(heavy cream with at least 35% fat)

MILK CHOCOLATE GANACHE

840g (30oz)   **Milk chocolate**
(with at least 30% cocoa solids)

280ml (10fl oz)   **Double cream**
(heavy cream with at least 35% fat)

DIRECTIONS

1. Chop the chocolate into very small pieces. The smaller the pieces, the easier it is to melt and combine with your hot cream. Place these shards in a heatproof bowl, such as a Pyrex®.

2. Pour the cream into a heavy-bottomed pot. If you planned to flavour the ganache, add any extracts or flavourings. Bring the cream just to a boil over a medium heat (it should only start to bubble). Immediately remove from the heat.

3. Pour the cream onto your chopped chocolate and briefly stir gently. After a couple of minutes, gently stir again to combine the melted chocolate and cream. If there are any pieces of chocolate remaining, let sit for another minute and stir again. Repeat this process until all the chocolate has melted and is fully combined with the cream.

4. The ganache will be liquid at this stage and will slowly harden as it cools. When it reaches the consistency of toothpaste, it's perfect for covering your cake.

5. If the ganache has cooled beyond the right consistency, you can microwave it on short bursts to melt it again—don't overheat it, as it may split. Due to the high percentage of cocoa solids, dark chocolate ganache is the most stable and the easiest to make. White chocolate ganache has a low percentage of cocoa solids and is the least stable and the most difficult to master.

BUTTERCREAM

Yield: Enough to cover and fill an 8" round cake (4" tall)
Prep time: 5 mins
Making time: 15 mins

Old faithful buttercream—you can't beat it! (Unless you're making it, then you need to beat it.) Experiment with flavours—the possibilities are endless! Add some instant coffee mixed with a little boiling water for coffee flavour. Pop in a couple of teaspoons of lemon zest and a little lemon juice for a citrus version. Or make a paste out of 3–4 tablespoons of cocoa powder and a bit of boiling water to make a chocolate version. This is a great basic recipe to get you started.

INGREDIENTS

227g (8oz)	**Unsalted butter** *(room temperature and soft)*
450g (16oz)	**Icing sugar** *(confectioner's sugar)*

DIRECTIONS

1. Use a stand mixer with the flat beater attachment to beat the butter until it's fluffy and pale. You can use a hand beater instead—it's just more work!

2. Sieve 1/3 of the icing sugar into the butter and beat until it's fully incorporated. Repeat until you've mixed in all of the icing sugar.

3. If the buttercream is too stiff, beat in a couple of teaspoons of boiling water to loosen it up and make it easier to work with.

GLOSSARY

Acetate — A firm, clear, plastic sheet often used to make chocolate cake wraps and to wrap chocolate biscuit cake.

Baking parchment — Used as a non-stick surface for baking. This paper is similar to wax paper but does not have a waxy coating.

Buttercream — A soft icing mix of butter and icing sugar used to fill or ice cakes.

Cake board — A board that is covered in foil and is around 3–4mm thick on which to place cakes.

Cake drum — A thick and more supportive version of a cake board that is made from cardboard or foam board that is around 12–13mm thick.

Calyx — The outer leaf-like part of a flower that opens to reveal the internal flower. Once the flower blooms, the calyx appear as small leaves growing from the flower's base.

CelBud — A cone-shaped polystyrene foam mould used as a centre for sugar-flower buds.

Clingfilm — A thin plastic film used for sealing and keeping food fresh. Also known as plastic wrap or Saran™ wrap.

Colouring gel — A concentrated food colouring that is thick and syrup-like.

Confectioner's glaze — An edible glaze (when dry) that is used to give a sheen to cakes, flowers, or models.

Confectioner's varnish — See above

Coupler — A tool used with piping bags to make a quick change between piping tips. It has two parts, one that is inserted into the tip of the pastry bag and another that screws onto it, securing the piping tip into place from the outside of the bag.

Dragée — A bite-sized candy with a hard outer shell. These candies are often used as a cake decoration.

Dresden tool — A popular double-ended cake tool used for marking and frilling petals and marking and detailing cakes.

Epiglottis (a.k.a. 'dangly bit') — This is the part of the body that flops down over the windpipe. It keeps food from going into your lungs.

Extruder — A sausage-making tool that is great for squeezing out strands of icing hair, grass, ropes, etc.

Flexi smoother — Flat, plastic, FDA-approved sheets that help create sharp edges on cakes.

Flood (flooding) — Filling in a section of cookie with a thin and runny icing.

Floral tape — A stretchable tape that comes in many colours. Used primarily for attaching sugar flower wires to create leaves and bouquets.

Florist wire A flexible aluminium wire coated with a thin layer of coloured paper. These wires are used for internal structure for figures and for the stems of sugar flowers. Available in a variety of gauges.

Flower veiner A silicone mould used to create the texture and veins of a flower's petals.

Fondant A thick sugary paste used to cover cakes.

Former Made from sugarpaste, it allows the roundedness of sugar heads to be maintained when working on facial features.

Ganache A tasty icing and filling for cakes made from chocolate and cream. It can be made from white, milk, or dark chocolate and can be used as is or whipped for a different texture.

Impression mat A silicone or plastic mat used to create textures in fondant, sugarpaste, or modelling chocolate.

Leaf veiner A silicone mould used to create the texture and veins of a flower's leaves.

Lustre dusts A type of decorating powder used to add sparkle and shimmer. Be careful because some types of lustres are not edible.

Palette knife A dull, thin blade with a handle for applying and spreading icings.

Parchment paper See baking parchment

Pith The spongy white tissue lining the rind of oranges, lemons, and other citrus fruits.

Piping couplers See Coupler.

Plastic wrap See Cling film.

Scribe (a.k.a. scribing tool, scriber needle) A needle-like tool, often used with a template to mark out designs onto cakes. In cookie decorating it is most often used to pop bubbles in royal icing.

Stitching wheel tool Quickly wheels a stitching pattern to modelled fabric.

Sugarpaste See Fondant

Torte Slicing a cake into layers.

Transfer (royal icing) Also known as run outs. This is a royal icing technique where a shape is piped onto parchment paper or acetate and allowed to dry; the shape can be peeled off and applied to cookies, cakes, etc.

Veining board A board with grooves in it to create the veining effect on sugar flower leaves.

Wet-on-wet A royal icing technique where the design is piped on while the base layer of the icing is still wet, allowing the design to dry flat and smooth.

X-Acto A small, sharp knife used in crafting. Also known as a blade.

INDEX

PHOTOGRAPHS

Cover
Tawin Island, Co. Galway
Corinna Maguire

Page 4
Cliffs of Moher, Co. Clare
Vincent Guth on Unsplash

Page 6
Cliffs of Moher, Co. Clare
Photo by Nils Nedel on Unsplash

Page 49
Connemara National Park
Robert Ruggiero on Unsplash

Page 122
The Dark Hedges
Photo by Trevor Cole on Unsplash

Notes